The
Eternal
Crossroads

The Art of

FLANNERY

O'CONNOR

Leon V. Driskell
& Joan T. Brittain

The University
Press of
Kentucky

Standard Book Number: 8131–1239–7

Library of Congress Catalog Card Number: 70–132828

Copyright © 1971 by The University Press of Kentucky

A statewide cooperative scholarly publishing agency
serving Berea College, Centre College of Kentucky,
Eastern Kentucky University, Kentucky State College,
Morehead State University, Murray State University,
University of Kentucky, University of Louisville,
and Western Kentucky University.

Editorial and Sales Offices: Lexington, Kentucky 40506

To Sue & to Bill

To Flannery O'Connor (1925-1964)

In August light, she began her night.
Closing her eyes, she let in the dark
Where light had burned so bright.
She left a legacy of burning rays,
Darkly to light the works of days.

If for her some welcome darkness
Came at last when she died,
We remain now in her greater light,
Ears dazzled by the Word she cried,
Eyes opened to let in the dark.

For now, a dark line of trees shivers
And moves, and we, like blind men cured,
See not trees but men, and they dance
The joy of a world of blind men cured,
As the bush quivers, kindles, flames.

> Her vision burns our virtues clean.

Out of darkness comes a burning light
To burn clean our eyes for the night
With signs of Grace in multiple eyes
Of spreading peacock tails, or in one
Glowing eye of the ever-constant sun,
Ivory-soft as the elevated Host,
But soaked in sunset blood.

> Her darkness is the only light.

L. V. D.

Contents

Acknowledgments

We are grateful to the Graduate Dean of the University of Louisville and to the Academic Dean of Bellarmine College for typing funds. We also thank Tom Kimmel and Fred Milne for patient and conscientious library assistance and Judy Cook and Rachel Thompson for typing.

Portions of this book have previously appeared in *Renascence, Georgia Review, Explicator,* and *Bulletin of Bibliography.* "To Flannery O'Connor (1925–1964)" is reprinted by permission of *Southern Humanities Review.* Grateful acknowledgment is made to the following publishers for permission to reprint: FARRAR, STRAUS & GIROUX, INC., for extracts from works by Flannery O'Connor—*Wise Blood,* copyright © 1952 by Flannery O'Connor; *The Violent Bear It Away,* copyright © 1960 by Flannery O'Connor; *Everything That Rises Must Converge,* copyright © 1965 by the Estate of Mary Flannery O'Connor; *Flannery O'Connor, Mystery and Manners: Occasional Prose,* selected and edited by Sally and Robert Fitzgerald, copyright © 1957, 1961, 1963, 1964, 1966, 1967, 1969 by the Estate of Mary Flannery O'Connor, copyright © 1962 by Flannery O'Connor, copyright © 1961 by Farrar, Straus and Cudahy, Inc.; and for extracts from François Mauriac, *The Weakling* and *The Enemy,* English translation copyright © 1952 by Pellegrini and Cudahy, Inc.; HARCOURT BRACE JOVANOVICH, INC., for extracts from Flannery O'Connor, *A Good Man Is Hard to Find and Other Stories,* copyright © 1953, 1954, 1955 by Flannery O'Connor; HARCOURT, BRACE & WORLD, INC., for extracts from T. S. Eliot, *Collected Poems 1909–1962;* HARPER & ROW, INC., for extracts from Pierre Teilhard de Chardin, *The Future of Man,* English translation copyright © 1964 by Harper & Row, Inc.; NEW LEADER, 23 June 1952, for extracts from Harvey C. Webster, "Nihilism As a Faith," copyright © 1952 by the American Labor Conference on International Affairs, Inc.

Preface

One of the "composites" Sally and Robert Fitzgerald include in *Mystery and Manners,* their collection of Flannery O'Connor's "occasional prose," is a piece with the unlikely sounding title "The Teaching of Literature." This composite includes Miss O'Connor's manuscript for a talk at a writers' conference (location unknown) and an article published in the *Georgia Bulletin.* It is one of the few essays in *Mystery and Manners* which we had not consulted in 1965 and 1966 when we first began close study of Miss O'Connor's fiction. Its appearance, after our work was done, has cheered us greatly, for every line of the following book is dedicated to the premise Miss O'Connor expresses in that essay: "the form of a story gives it meaning which any other form would change."

As teachers and writers, we came to our work with Miss O'Connor's fiction convinced also of the truth of her claim that "unless the student is able, in some degree, to apprehend the form, he will never apprehend anything else about the work, except what is extrinsic to it as literature." It is almost as if Miss O'Connor, whose death in 1964 saddened us and hundreds of other readers, had personally commended our method of treating her novels and stories. For though we are ourselves native Georgians and think we share with Miss O'Connor a part of our region's ambience, we have sought largely to exclude "what is extrinsic to [her work] as literature." We have been concerned with her stories as stories and as form, not as regional or sectarian formulations; we have not presumed to "understand" Miss O'Connor in any except literary terms, nor have we tried to rip out her themes as easy explanations of the mystery embodied in her stories.

We have sought to interpret and evaluate the whole of Miss O'Connor's fictional achievement in what we regard as more inclusive terms than other critics have done. In 1966 at the University of Louisville Mrs. Brittain had completed her M.A. thesis, in which she stressed the formal coherence and artistry of Miss O'Connor's works, not the regional grotesquerie so often observed by critics then. The emphasis of Mrs. Brittain's work, "Symbols of Violence: Flannery O'Connor's Structure of Reality," was almost entirely ontological, but it performed other vital scholarly chores as well: for example, her thesis indicated for the first time the extent to which Miss O'Connor revised short pieces for inclusion in her novels and in her collections. Furthermore, Mrs. Brittain's bibliography was the most thorough in existence when she submitted it to *Bulletin of Bibliography,* where it appeared in three parts.

The Eternal Crossroads, an extension of Mrs. Brittain's thesis, represents our mutual admiration and respect for Miss O'Connor as an artist as well as our delight in her written words. Our pleasure in the stories has not diminished with our preparation of manuscript and the necessary attentiveness to the demands of scholarship.

After several years of work, though continuing to avoid excessive reliance upon the facts of Miss O'Connor's life, we have attempted to place her works in perspective, to establish several major literary and theological influences, and to demonstrate the effect of those influences upon specific works. In particular, we have demonstrated that the French novelist François Mauriac provided Miss O'Connor with ideas and images which—consciously or subconsciously—she made peculiarly her own. Initially she had tried, as she admitted, to "take over" the problems of Mauriac, and that effort delayed her finding her own fictional voice. Our work traces her literary and doctrinal progression from what she regarded as excessive reliance on Mauriac, forward to her acceptance of the optimistic and idealistic Christology of another great French writer: Pierre Teilhard de Chardin.

The change in Miss O'Connor's belief is not dramatic; nor do her stories change drastically: her published works are remarkably uniform in quality. Yet, as she enriched her faith through an increasingly positive sense of the redemption, her stories achieved greater luster. We regard her last stories as fulfillment of earlier promise.

The organization of this book is simple: from establishment of Miss O'Connor's major literary influences we have proceeded to a chronological examination of all her published works, concentrating always on the essential unity and pervasive artistry of the whole.

CHAPTER ONE

The Eternal Crossroads

IN ONE of her essays, "The Regional Writer," Flannery O'Connor spoke of "the peculiar crossroads where time and place and eternity somehow meet." Though Miss O'Connor's task as a writer was to find the location of that "peculiar crossroads," her personal crossroads was Andalusia, her Georgia farmhouse near Milledgeville, where she lived with her widowed mother and indulged her fancy for raising poultry. The world came often to Andalusia, and most of the visitors took away at least one peacock feather as well as respect for Miss O'Connor's unpretentious and frequently wry humor.

Like another unmarried American woman writer, Emily Dickinson, Flannery O'Connor expanded the boundaries of her experience through imagination and through the happy faculties of realizing the importance of things and places, of relating the local to the cosmic. Both women grounded their work in reality and so remained safe from writing about ideas as such, but Miss O'Connor was less restricted to Andalusia than her predecessor had been restricted to Amherst.

For a time Flannery O'Connor studied at the University of Iowa's creative writing program, where she probably learned most of the literary theory at her disposal, and later she lived with Robert and Sally Fitzgerald in Connecticut. But illness sent her home to Georgia, and except for brief trips she lived there for the remaining thirteen years of her life, until her death in August 1964, just short of her fortieth birthday. At the urging of her cousin Katie, she and her mother joined a group of Savannah pilgrims to go to Lourdes, where her mother and cousin doubtless hoped she would enjoy a cure of the blood disease, lupus, which threatened her life and which had killed her father. That sojourn and lecture trips to a surprisingly large number of colleges and universities constituted her travel after 1952. During the brief span between 1952 and 1964 she did the bulk of her writing.

In those few years of her active career, often plagued by illness, Miss O'Connor produced two remarkable short novels and a score of classic short stories. At the same time she also worked out a personal credo of art and life.[1] Although she did not—and probably could not—separate the theory of fiction from the practice of fiction, just as she could not separate the facts of her regional origin and her religious faith from her life as an artist, she began during her last years to speak more directly and clearly of her approach to writing and of the role of place and religion in her work.

Miss O'Connor's characters, nearly all of them Georgians, embody her search for a location at which the exigencies of time and place are related to eternity. Though her characters, with a few notable exceptions, are literate only in the narrowest sense of the word, they are nevertheless capable of experiencing what she called the South's "vision of Moses' face as he pulverized our idols." Through these characters Miss O'Connor has given body and substance to her region, for as she well understood, the southern writer "is not a writer who goes away and can't go home again, or someone who stays and is not quite appreciated, but someone who is a part of what he writes about and is recognized as such." Flannery O'Connor was no outsider, no alien concerned primarily with expressing the agony of mutual rejection. She was a Georgia writer doing what all writers must do, seeking to locate the intersection of the universal with her own time and place. Rarely did she speak in such grandiose terms, but she has said enough about her art to reveal that she recognized the essentially personal and individual aspects of the writer's vision.

More important, she recognized that stories "of any depth" always deal with fundamental human issues. Her stories are cosmic, dealing, as she herself said, with matters of life and death; this they do in a way that permits the reader to participate in the experience rather than merely witness a performance. They are also comic in the finest sense of the word.

She was impatient with topics such as "the health of the novel," which she regarded as schoolteacher talk. She was immune to the

literary trade with its jargon, its catering to the current taste. She recognized that some writers, critics, and editors prefer to flock to fads,
creating and praising fiction not influenced by the outside world at
all—only by television. New York critics, for example, she called "an
unreliable lot," no matter how friendly, for "they are as incapable as
on the day they were born of interpreting Southern literature to the
world." The critics, though necessary, chilled her with their habits of
collecting what others of their kind have said—collecting sometimes
carelessly, sometimes meticulously, but nearly always without passion, without vigor, and with no sense of what Miss O'Connor would
have been unashamed to call "what they can testify to."

Writing about what she could testify to, Miss O'Connor preferred
also to talk about that, rather than about fashions and trends in fiction, influences and techniques. (This is not to say that she was unaware of technique or ignorant of the way the artist shapes a tale or
another source to convey his own peculiar theme in dramatic form.)
Though willing to sneer at the intellectual, the purveyor of clichés
and formulae, abstracted and bloodless, she did not sneer at the religious intensity of her part of the world, where the people she knew
fell generally into two groups—the fanatics and the others. The critics who see her characters yielding before the madness of fanaticism
and assume that the author deplores such madness know neither Miss
O'Connor nor her region; she recognized the "incredible innocence"
which permitted H. L. Mencken scornfully to call the South the
Bible Belt. She also recognized the truth of Walker Percy's claim that
the existence of a great many good southern writers resulted from the
fact that "we lost the war" and that "behind our own history, deepening at every point, has been another history." For Miss O'Connor
two truths came together at a peculiar crossroads: "Not every lost
war would have this effect on every society, but we were doubly
blessed, not only in our Fall, but in having a means to interpret it."
For her, Appomattox and its aftermath assumed metaphysical implications comparable to those William Blake saw in the American and
French revolutions. Eternity, not time, is the context in which both
writers interpret the human drama.

Her awareness of "another history" and of the added dimension of
eternity made her an alien in the sense that she was isolated from the
twentieth-century secular society. The South, with its history and

legend, including its loss of the war, aches with the sense of its fall; its guilt goes marching on. The Detroit truckdriver who gives one of Miss O'Connor's characters a ride knows that he will meet no sane person until he gets back to Detroit. Her South is a region of peculiar people, men and women set apart by awareness of their own difference; their history has its ultimate meaning in Holy Writ, not in statistics, nor in the "sciences of adjustment" so important to most of her contemporaries.

Furthermore, though Miss O'Connor identifies herself with the fanatics rather than with the others, she belonged by accident of birth to a minority group, a Roman Catholic community in fundamentalist Georgia; this fact necessarily created an irony in her religious images, for the symbols of the Roman Catholic faith cannot be applied without wrenching to the quests of her fundamentalist characters. In part, then, her Catholicism also cut her off from the fullest participation in the life of her community; she was different even in a region of people who prided themselves in their difference. But her sympathy with her fundamentalist characters, her willingness to side with them against the rest of the world, is everywhere apparent in her fiction. Though critics have not hesitated to assume the madness of O'Connor characters such as old Mason Tarwater, the writer herself told Granville Hicks that she was behind Tarwater "one hundred percent."

Admitting that her sense of morality and normality springs from Christian orthodoxy and from her belief that "Christ should be the center of life and the individual soul," she wrote that "the most obvious thing about the society I live in and write about is that Christ is hardly the center of it. Even in the 'Bible Belt' where I come from, Christ only haunts us from the fringes. I am a Catholic living in a society that is normally Protestant but isn't even that with much vigor any more." Writers who see from a religious point of view, she recognized, "will tend to certain violences of expression and form to get [their] vision across to what [they] take to be a hostile audience." Furthermore, "writers who do believe in religious realities and propose to get them across in fiction have to cope with a deaf, dumb, and blind reader; and the grotesque may be one of our desperate answers."[2]

Miss O'Connor's "desperate answers," her grotesques, have led some readers to judge her work as despairing, but she vehemently denied this in an interview with Gerard E. Sherry, maintaining that "my characters are described as despairing only by superficial critics. Very few of my characters despair and those who do, don't reflect my views. You have to get the writer's view by looking at the novel as a whole."[3] Ever since the critics began to take notice of Miss O'Connor's works, they have emphasized the grotesque qualities in the stories, apparently judging that what is different from the norm falls necessarily into the category of the grotesque.[4] Some Georgians, including the authors of this study, maintain that the people who best understand Flannery O'Connor's work see nothing grotesque about it at all: they see only that she has captured important elements of life as it is and that her regional peculiarities are true of all regions in varying degrees.

The pervasiveness of her faith, her desire for a Christ-centered world, not one haunted by Christ from the fringes, obliged Miss O'Connor to seek inner, or spiritual, progress rather than external, or social, progress. In short, as Thomas Quinn has recently observed, Miss O'Connor's religion was largely Augustinian in contrast to C. S. Lewis's Anglo-Catholicism, which runs closer to Thomistic thought.[5] Perhaps because of her Augustinianism, social reform, even the struggle for racial justice, did not usually touch her very deeply.

Her fiction does not seek to accomplish the aims of satire: the ordinary Georgians she wrote about even when she was away from home —her poor people, her ignorant backwoodsmen—are not there to incite our sympathy or to urge specific social action. They are there precisely because they are there and thus have significant human and religious meaning; they make real her "realm of mystery." (Asked why she used the sun as a symbol so often, Miss O'Connor replied with characteristic practicality, "Because it's always there.")

Unlike Erskine Caldwell, whose works have a certain polemical value, Miss O'Connor did not write about Negro-white relations in the South for the sake of encouraging change or dramatizing inequity. When her people say "nigger," it is without passion: they are naming one of the realities of their lives. She may speak for more of the South than has generally been admitted when she denies the impact of integration on the region; in her interview with Gerard Sherry she said that Negroes and whites have always milled around together and "now they can mill around in a few more places."

Rarely does she make the Negro-white relationship central to a story; never does she attempt to develop a Negro character, for as a white woman, a product of the segregated South, she recognized that she could not get inside Negro characters. Nevertheless, she did use the facts of her region effectively, albeit without the reformer's zeal. For example, in "The Artificial Nigger" Mr. Head's and Nelson's common racial arrogance serves the cause of grace, and a battered figure of an "artificial nigger" comes to embody the suffering of humanity. Her early stories "The Geranium" and "The Train," both later reworked, reveal a preoccupation with Negro-white relationships to which she returned in rewriting "The Geranium" and in writing "Everything That Rises Must Converge." These stories, dealing with the South's changing social order, provide the framework of her final collection.

So far Miss O'Connor has largely been interpreted by critics who do not understand the universality of her experiences as a Georgian or as a Catholic. Although her works have relevance to readers who do not share her origins or her religion, these readers constitute a part of that "hostile audience" of which she spoke. They negate Miss O'Connor's vision by localizing it and then by refusing to take into account the facts of the region. A writer for *Atlanta* magazine (August 1963) quoted Miss O'Connor's statement that "one uses a region in order to suggest what transcends it" and then added: "Her own unflinching gaze extends beyond problems and paraphernalia to 'that realm of mystery which is the concern of prophets.' " "Readers who miss this point," the author continues, "seldom get beyond the regional grotesqueries of Miss O'Connor's work" (p. 63).

The late Thomas Merton came closer to the mark in his tribute to Miss O'Connor: "When I read Flannery, I don't think of Hemingway, or Katherine Anne Porter, or Sartre, but rather of someone like Sophocles. What more can you say of a writer? I write her name with honor, for all the truth and all the craft with which she shows man's fall and his dishonor."[6] Secular humanism would seek to explain and thus mitigate "man's fall and his dishonor." The larger tradition, however, has been content to dramatize the fact of the fall: the beginning of tragedy and truth for Oedipus occurs at the crossroads where, seeking to escape his destiny, he fulfills it through murdering the king his father.

Just as the Oedipus story contributed elements to Miss O'Connor's first novel, so the idea of the crossroads seems pervasive in her work and in her idea of literature generally. Another southern woman writer, Eudora Welty, expressed an idea similar to Miss O'Connor's "peculiar crossroads" when she wrote that the "crossroads of circumstances" are the "proving grounds of 'what happened? Who's here? Who's coming?' "[7] This Mississippi writer also shared Miss O'Connor's belief in the importance of place, for she insisted that "fiction depends for its life on place."

Another novelist, John Hawkes, in an essay called "Flannery O'Connor's Devil," recognized the "peculiar crossroads" in Miss O'Connor's tendency to combine in her work, "in a mercilessly pleasureable tension," a sense of the "unknown country" and of "actuality." Even more to the point, Hawkes put in focus Miss O'Connor's evocation of mystery. Hawkes and Nathan Scott, Jr., were among the few critics who recognized, before the publication of *Mystery and Manners,* her essentially anagogical method.[8] After *Mystery and Manners* appeared, D. Keith Mano was among the reviewers to recognize the importance of the anagogical, or, in his words, the "pervasive sense of Grace, of the Divine inhering in the things of the world."[9]

Miss O'Connor's most explicit statement about the anagogical method appears in her essay "The Nature and Aim of Fiction," where she wrote: "The kind of vision the fiction writer needs to have or to develop, in order to increase the meaning of his story is called anagogical vision, and that is the kind of vision that is able to see different levels of reality in one image or one situation." She expanded her definition by citing the three kinds of meaning medieval commentators found within the literal level of Scripture: allegorical, tropological, and anagogical. She added, "Although this was a method applied to biblical exegesis, it was also an attitude toward all of creation, and a way of reading nature which included most possibilities, and I think it is this enlarged view of the human scene that the fiction writer has to cultivate" (*Mystery and Manners,* pp. 72–73).

In her essay "The Teaching of Literature," from which Sally and Robert Fitzgerald drew their collection's title, *Mystery and Manners,* Miss O'Connor stipulates that the fiction writer is concerned with "ultimate mystery as we find it embodied in the concrete world of sense experience." Furthermore, "Since this is his aim, all levels of meaning in fiction have come increasingly to be found in the literal level. There is no room for abstract expressions of compassion or piety or morality in the fiction itself. This means that the writer's moral sense must coincide with his dramatic sense, and this makes the presentation to the student, and particularly to the immature student, very difficult indeed" (p. 125).

In a talk at Sweetbriar College in March 1963, Miss O'Connor reminded her listeners that St. Augustine "wrote that the things of the world pour forth from God in a double way: intellectually into the minds of the angels and physically into the world of things." In that lecture, published in *Mystery and Manners* as "Novelist and Believer," she continued:

> To the person who believes this—as the western world did up until a few centuries ago—this physical, sensible world is good because it proceeds from a divine source. The artist usually knows this by instinct; his senses, which are used to penetrating the concrete, tell him so. When Conrad said that his aim as an artist was to render the highest possible justice to the visible universe, he was speaking with the novelist's surest instinct. The artist penetrates the concrete world in order to find at its depths the image of its source, the image of ultimate reality. This, in no way hinders his perception of evil, but rather sharpens it, for only when the natural world is seen as good does evil becomes intelligible as a destructive force and a necessary result of our freedom.
>
> (p. 157)

Nathan Scott strikes to the heart of the matter with the observation that "mystery is not the unknown but, rather, that surplusage of meaning in what is known." Hence, as he recognizes in his essay "Flannery O'Connor's Testimony," mystery is not "something that arises out of the perceptual process itself; mystery is not, in other words, a name for a merely subjective reality." Scott interprets mystery as an ontological category. Relying in part upon terms and ideas from Abraham J. Heschel's *Between God and Man*, he continues: "[Mystery] speaks not of anything foisted upon the world by the human imagination but of a 'most powerful presence beyond the mind' which makes for 'a fundamental norm of human consciousness.' It is not something which we infer from a psychological reaction but rather that to which the *sense* of mystery, of wonder, of amazement, is a response."[10]

Miss O'Connor and several of her most outspoken characters (notably old Tarwater) would hasten to support his denial that mystery arises as a quirk of the human imagination. She expressed in several of her essays in *Mystery and Manners* her repugnance at Manichaeanism, the almost perennial heresy which separates spirit from matter. She does so with particular effectiveness in "The Nature and Aim of Fiction," where she suggests that the modern spirit and the "sensibility infected with it" also seek "pure spirit" and try "to approach the infinite directly without any mediation of matter." Under such circumstances, she writes, "fiction is hard if not impossible to write because fiction is so very much an incarnational art." Implicitly denying the subjective basis of mystery, she writes in her next paragraph of the "common and sad spectacle . . . of a person of really fine sensibility and acute psychological perception trying to write fiction by using these qualities alone" (*Mystery and Manners*, p. 68).

Possibly the most serious barrier to some readers' grasp of Miss O'Connor's fiction is its lack of "elevation," or what she wryly called "uplift." For her "the materials of the fiction writer are the humblest." Everyday objects are dignified with meaning, and at her "peculiar crossroads," or at Eudora Welty's "crossroads of circumstances," the writer's moral sense coincides with his dramatic sense to create the threefold meaning (allegorical, tropological, and anagogical) which makes statement of theme largely irrelevant.

In "Writing Short Stories," a lecture she read at a writers' conference, Miss O'Connor observes: "People talk about the theme of a story as if the theme were like the string that a sack of chicken feed is tied with. They think that if you can pick out the theme, the way you pick the right thread in the chicken-feed sack, you can rip the story open and feed the chickens. But this is not the way meaning works in fiction." She adds that "when you can state the theme of a story, when you can separate it from the story itself, then you can be sure the story is not a very good one." Furthermore, and most explicitly, "The meaning of a story has to be embodied in it, has to be made concrete in it" (*Mystery and Manners*, p. 96).

Exactly: Miss O'Connor created mystery through manners, by

which she meant the conventions of her art. At her best, she is beyond paraphrase and thematic summation, for her stories do more than dramatize themes: they structure reality.

Unfortunately, *Time*'s reviewer of *A Good Man Is Hard to Find* did not recognize that Miss O'Connor's gaze extended to the mysterious realm "which is the concern of prophets," for the review speaks of "ten witheringly sarcastic stories" set in a South that moves along a "sort of up-to-date Tobacco Road paved right into town" (6 June 1955, p. 114). This reading represents the early majority view; as Sister Bertrande writes in *Esprit*'s memorial issue to Miss O'Connor, real understanding of her work awaited the appearance of Miss O'Connor's essay "The Fiction Writer and His Country" in Granville Hicks's *The Living Novel* (New York: Macmillan, 1957).

Summing up attitudes toward Miss O'Connor's work, Sister Bertrande writes of "an uncertainty . . . a reserved appreciation" of the author's "perceptiveness" and, from those who favored her work, "an acceptance . . . that she was skilled in drawing unusual portraits of unusual characters." On the other hand, Miss O'Connor's detractors were ready with "all sorts of accusations about her penchant for freaks." Finally, according to Sister Bertrande, "almost as if constrained to do so, Flannery spoke up for herself. In seven pages of unassailable logic . . . Flannery brings into sharp focus the import of her fiction: 'I am no disbeliever in spiritual purpose . . . and I am no vague believer. I see from the standpoint of Christian orthodoxy.' "[11]

Miss O'Connor's protestation of Christian orthodoxy at least provided a starting place for the critics to get at her works. However, even if one is willing to accept her statement of faith and her regional origins, he cannot grasp the full meaning of her fiction unless he undertakes the arduous task of readjusting his sight to her terms. Her work will reward the ordinary reader, the one little concerned with meanings beyond the obvious, with the kind of reality which would be misnamed if called realism; it will provide the frequent laugh and the constant grimace of recognition at human foibles, for Flannery O'Connor's genius is as much comic as it is cosmic.[12]

She recognized, however, that a reading public unaccustomed to reading the Bible and lost in a "haze of compassion" would fail to understand her completely. To pity her characters, and merely to pity them, is to do both them and her an injustice. One must recognize that death and physical suffering are not the worst evils in her universe: "I'm a born Catholic," she told C. Ross Mullins, "and death has always been brother to my imagination." The facts of her life may have made the necessity of preparing for a good death (in the Catholic sense) a personal obsession with her; at any rate, her stories usually conclude with death or its foreshadowing, but we are not to despair at death. The reader's task is to examine the manner and circumstances of her characters' deaths, for death often provides their only hope.

Miss O'Connor's Catholicism no less than her affinity for Bible Belt fundamentalists makes knowledge of the Bible important for her readers. The prominence of the Bible in her fiction is a result of her awareness that southern history is not only a part of western civilization's history but that it can also be seen as an extension of that other history which is the Bible; she made this clear in her essay "The Regional Writer."

Biblical allusion functions in her work in several ways. An individual story's full significance may depend upon the reader's recognition of an allusion. For instance, The Tower, the barbecue joint in "A Good Man Is Hard to Find," should bring to mind the Tower of Babel. Understanding the collection in which this story appears requires a similar awareness, for the good man sought throughout the collection and found at the end in Mr. Guizac, the DP of "The Displaced Person," appears in fulfillment of prophecy: he is the "one good man," the ransom foretold in the Old Testament. In short, recognition of allusions and awareness of the relationship between the opening and the concluding stories enable the reader to redefine goodness and to perceive that Guizac's goodness goes far beyond the secular standard discussed at The Tower.

Another influence upon Miss O'Connor was the work of Teilhard de Chardin. This influence is difficult to assess because her knowledge of Teilhard came late in her life and because his ideas in many ways replaced and in other ways extended those ideas of Catholic orthodoxy which had shaped all her life's work. According to Robert Fitzgerald's introduction to *Everything That Rises Must Converge*, she had been reading Teilhard "at least since early 1961" (p. xxx). Every one of the stories in that collection affirms the positive and redemptive nature of the Christian faith, and the structure of the collection also serves to emphasize the theme of redemption.

Though interpreting the ideas of Teilhard de Chardin must await full analysis of *Everything That Rises Must Converge,* it is appropriate here to note that the Jesuit paleontologist developed in his work the idea of a constantly evolving universe. Undismayed by the physical facts of evolution, Teilhard insisted that man is in the process of rising spiritually as well as physically: the climax of his vision is the perfection of the universe into a "thinking universe," the fullest expression of humanity, which is the Body of Christ.

Many events doubtless prepared Miss O'Connor for her final acceptance of Teilhard's ideas. Her physical illness, for instance, may have led her to regard death itself in a more personal, less abstract way than she did earlier. And Pope John's innovations and liberalizations within the Roman Catholic Church coincided with social alterations in Miss O'Connor's native South. Her acceptance of such changes and her recognition that physical, psychological, and social improvements may be part of spiritual evolution led her to soften her distinctions between internal and external progress. She came, in short, to recognize the dependence of the spiritual upon other aspects of life. No matter what personal experiences were involved, her awareness converged to bring her to a very nearly mystical acceptance of Teilhard's ideas.

Miss O'Connor's early works typically bring her characters to revelations of a highly personal sort, out of which hope of redemption arises. In the later works she dramatizes their arrival at Teilhard's "point omega," where they achieve significant gains in spiritual energy. These gains result from recognition of their relations to other people, and, appropriately, they lead inevitably to fuller awareness of individual human identity.

In an interview with John Enck in 1963, John Hawkes included Flannery O'Connor among writers of the avant-garde, specifying that, for him, avant-garde "has to do with something constant which we find running through prose fiction from Quevedo, the Spanish picaresque writer, and Thomas Nashe at the beginnings of the English novel, down through Lautréamont, Céline, Nathanael West, Flannery O'Connor, James Purdy, Joseph Heller, myself." His explanation of the constant in avant-garde writing provides insight to

Flannery O'Connor's place in American fiction: "This constant is a quality of coldness, detachment, ruthless determination to face up to the enormities of ugliness and potential failure within ourselves and in the world around us, and to bring to this exposure a savage or saving comic spirit and the saving beauties of language."[13]

Miss O'Connor's introduction to *A Memoir of Mary Ann* suggests a similar point of view:

> In popular pity, we mark our gain in sensibility and our loss in vision. If other ages felt less, they saw more, even though they saw with the blind, prophetical unsentimental eye of acceptance, which is to say, of faith. In the absence of this faith now, we govern by tenderness. It is a tenderness which, long since cut off from the person of Christ, is wrapped in theory. When tenderness is detached from the source of tenderness, its logical outcome is terror. It ends in forced-labor camps and in the fumes of the gas chamber.
>
> (*Mystery and Manners*, p. 227)

Flannery O'Connor's was not a vocation to compassionate evil into mere nongood but to permit a return to clear sight: "the blind, prophetical unsentimental eye of acceptance, which is to say, of faith."

CHAPTER TWO

Specific Influences:
Mauriac, Hawthorne, & West

BECAUSE Miss O'Connor's use of the Bible is constant and because the overall meaning of her work so nearly parallels the thought of Teilhard de Chardin, we will examine biblical influence in conjunction with individual analyses of stories and will conclude our study with an examination of her response to Teilhard. Meantime, however, assessment of three other influences on Miss O'Connor—François Mauriac, Nathaniel Hawthorne, and Nathanael West —is no less necessary than logical at this point, for those influences relate specifically to aspects of her structure and style as well as to her birth as an artist and her adoption of her characteristic images and symbols.

Miss O'Connor once stated, "I feel more of a kinship with Hawthorne than with any other American writer."[1] However, Mauriac is doubtless the most important of the three. He is almost certainly the writer from whom she learned the most—not technically but in terms of what she could "testify to." Specifically, Mauriac's short novel *Le Sagouin* (published in English in 1952 as *The Weakling*) seems to be the work which struck fire from Miss O'Connor's imagination and permitted the creation of the stories we regard today as representative of her best early work.

John Hawkes has suggested Nathanael West as an influence on Miss O'Connor. West's influence is almost exclusively superficial, observable in the correspondence Sabbath Lily opens with the lovelorn columnist toward the end of *Wise Blood*. Were it not for other similarities in Miss O'Connor's and West's works, one might posit that she could as well have drawn the idea for the correspondence from

Evelyn Waugh's *The Loved One*. (It is worth adding in support of Evelyn Waugh's possible influence on *Wise Blood* that the hero of *The Loved One* seeks to establish himself as a nondenominational clergyman. He expects to support himself and his bride-to-be by reading funeral services at the expensive cemetery where she is already employed. Her infatuation with the art of mortuary cosmetics and her identification with the dead, not the living, parallel Sabbath Lily's apparently maternal affection for the bloodless mummy in *Wise Blood*.)

Although West's influence on Miss O'Connor was neither pervasive nor deep, one should observe that, despite his Jewish origins, his books dramatize an essentially Christian quest, as suggested by his terming *Miss Lonelyhearts* "a portrait of a priest of our time who has had a religious experience." The irony of the comment requires no explanation, but perhaps one should remark that the religious experience is central, as has been established in James F. Light's analysis of the book.[2]

West—like Waugh and Miss O'Connor—worked largely in the short novel form; like them also, he generated a world of violence. Indeed he regarded violence in America as "idiomatic": European writers "need hundreds of pages to motivate one little murder. But not so the American writer."[3] West would certainly have enjoyed readers' protests over Miss O'Connor's cavalier treatment of legalism in her baptismal drowning of Bishop in *The Violent Bear It Away*.

Robert Fitzgerald has expressed surprise that the critics have overlooked the marked similarities between *Miss Lonelyhearts* and *Wise Blood*. An incidental similarity is that the triangular faces of West's characters appear on Miss O'Connor's people. In *Wise Blood*, for instance, a little girl with "long wood-shaving curls and a fierce triangular face" approaches Gonga, the gorilla star, to shake hands. Elsewhere, Miss O'Connor seems fond of emphasizing the sharpness of faces, as in the description of the salesman in *The Violent Bear It Away* who has a "narrow face that appeared to have been worn down to the sharpest possible depressions."

One of West's triangular-faced characters, Shrike (the "joke-machine"), works at the newspaper with the protagonist, Miss Lonelyhearts; Miss Lonelyhearts originally adopted his unlikely name as a joke but later began to take his correspondence seriously. Shrike relates himself to Miss Lonelyhearts in the same way Enoch Emery relates himself to Haze Motes in *Wise Blood*. Just as Haze, who is almost totally divorced from the world, is killed and later serves as an illuminating force for his landlady, so Miss Lonelyhearts dies to the world (to use Light's term) before physically dying at the hands of the cripple Doyle, whom he wishes to help. Thus, though destroyed, he serves to help his girlfriend Betty to a fuller, more satisfactory view of the world. Denying or ignoring the existence of violence and evil, Betty had enjoyed an oversimplified world in which Christ had no place. By ending Miss Lonelyhearts's quest, West begins Betty's initiation into the real meaning of life, for, pregnant with the child of the man she sees murdered, she can no longer cling to her perfect but futile vision. Betty's plight is similar to that in which Mauriac and Miss O'Connor frequently leave their characters: she is stripped of defenses and possibly made ready for acceptance of religious faith.

Despite these similarities between *Miss Lonelyhearts* and *Wise Blood*, one must regard Nathanael West's influence upon Miss O'Connor as secondary, or even tertiary, for there remain the far more extensive influences of Hawthorne and Mauriac. Miss O'Connor's statement of literary kinship with Hawthorne and her obvious familiarity with his work oblige the critic to seek evidence of direct influence, though the usual views of the New England "Puritan" appear to make it unlikely. Certainly the Georgia-born Roman Catholic seems, at first glance, to have little in common with Hawthorne. First impressions notwithstanding, Miss O'Connor's "Mary Ann: The Story of a Little Girl" helps to establish Hawthorne's importance to her as an author and as a man.

"Mary Ann: The Story of a Little Girl" first appeared in *Jubilee* and later as the introduction to a book written by a group of nuns.[4] Miss O'Connor's introduction links Hawthorne and his story "The Birthmark" with Mary Ann and the nuns who cared for her at Our Lady of Perpetual Help Free Cancer Home in Atlanta. The connection is the more credible because Hawthorne's daughter Rose became a nun and founded the order which cared for Mary Ann and which—more important in Miss O'Connor's eyes—taught her how to die.

Hawthorne's literary importance to Flannery O'Conner was largely technical, though her responses to the man himself and to the fact of his daughter's connection with Mary Ann elicited important statements from her about religion and literature. Although it is probable that Miss O'Connor drew some specific images from Hawthorne, it is beyond doubt that the author of *The Scarlet Letter* is her master in matters of structure. Furthermore, the two shared more beliefs about the human condition than most readers would assume possible.

The perfect arch structure of *The Scarlet Letter* provides a schema from which Miss O'Connor, consciously or otherwise, patterned both her novels and both her collections, for Hawthorne's novel employs the same reversal technique which typifies Miss O'Connor's books. The three scaffold scenes in *The Scarlet Letter* provide adequate evidence of the authors' structural similarities. Chapter two ("The Market Place") marks the first occurrence of the scaffold in Hawthorne's book; it is midday and Hester Prynne faces the people. The third scaffold scene (chapter twenty-two, the book's next to last chapter) also occurs at midday; Dimmesdale preaches from the scaffold in the marketplace. The second scaffold scene, the central or arch scene, occurs in chapter twelve; after this scene the reversal of events begins. Thus the three scaffold scenes represent dramatization of the apparent situation, the turning point, and resolution of the actual situation.

As individual analyses of the books will reveal, Miss O'Connor also employs a reversal technique in her fiction. In *Wise Blood* the three confrontations with caged animals correspond to Hawthorne's scaffold scenes. In the second novel, *The Violent Bear It Away,* the three baptismal scenes fill the same function. The quest for a good man and for truth begins in the title story of *A Good Man Is Hard to Find* and reaches its climax in the final story, "The Displaced Person." Finally, the existential plight of man in a world of guilt and sorrow begins with the title story of *Everything That Rises Must Converge* and is resolved with an otherworldly vision in the concluding story, "Judgement Day."

In the opening paragraph of "The New Adam and Eve" Hawthorne expresses succinctly some of the issues with which he and his literary kinswoman were concerned: "We who are born into the world's artificial system can never adequately know how little in our present state and circumstance is natural and how much is merely the interpolation of the perverted heart and mind of man. . . . It is only through the medium of the imagination that we can lessen those iron fetters which we call truth and reality, and make ourselves even partially sensible of what prisoners we are."[5]

Elsewhere in Hawthorne's work, in *The Marble Faun,* Miriam, referring to Donatello's experience of human sin, says that "he has travelled in a circle . . . and now comes back to his original self, with an inestimable treasure of improvement won from an experience of pain."[6] Her question, "Was the crime a blessing in disguise?" brings one to recognition of Hawthorne's belief, with O'Connor, that salvation is for sinners. The fall—as Haze Motes knows—implies a plan for redemption.

Miss O'Connor's work is full of complacent materialists who discover greater truths and realities than those they subscribe to daily; their recognition of the extent of their imprisonment and of their perversion leads to revelations of grace. The dreams about coffins, the confrontations with caged animals, the apparent necessity with which characters do evil, the conflicts of secularists and believers—all these and other elements of Miss O'Connor's fiction reveal the extent to which her view of man's fallen state corresponds with Hawthorne's. Above all, she saw with him the exaggeration of scientism which prevailed in his day and still prevails, and, as he did, she resorted to the medium of the imagination to "lessen those iron fetters which we call truth and reality."

Among other specific symbols probably drawn from Hawthorne's work, one must include the recurrent symbol of spectacles, the frequency of which is apparent in analyses of both writers' works and is discussed in Mrs. Brittain's essay "The Fictional Family of Flannery O'Connor." In "The Custom House" section of *The Scarlet Letter,* Hawthorne typifies his "good old gentlemen" morally and physically by defining their "vision." Their eyes "sagaciously, under their spectacles, did . . . peep into the holds of the vessels! Mighty was their fuss about little matters, and marvellous, sometimes, the obtuseness that allowed greater ones to slip between their fingers!"[7] The Cynic in Hawthorne's "The Great Carbuncle" joins in the search for the gem in order to prove that it does not exist; his spectacles are of considerable importance in the story, reminding the O'Connor reader that both the Misfit and Haze Motes wear silver-rimmed spectacles and that both are seeking truth by denying revealed religion. The Misfit looks defenseless without his glasses, and Haze cannot "see" until after he has flung his mother's glasses (his inherited faith) aside. Similarly, Hawthorne's Cynic raves that the gem is all humbug, and when the party reaches its goal, he asks, " 'Where is your Great Humbug? . . . I challenge you to make me see it.' 'There!' said Matthew, incensed at such perverse blindness, and turning the Cynic round towards the illuminated cliff. 'Take off those abominable spectacles and you cannot help seeing it.' " The Cynic is blinded when he views the great carbuncle, and, "having cast aside his spectacles, wandered about the world a miserable object, and was punished with an agonizing desire for light, for the willful blindness of his former life."[8] The patrolman in *Wise Blood* tells Haze he will be able to see better if he gets out of the car; once he has left the automobile and has seen it plunge over the embankment, Haze realizes the truth that he is not going anywhere and returns home to Mrs. Flood's house to blind himself. Only then can he truly "see."

Mr. Jerger in O'Connor's "A Stroke of Good Fortune" speaks of the Fountain of Youth and implies that he has found it in his heart; Dr. Heidegger in Hawthorne's "Dr. Heidegger's Experiment" tells Widow Wycherly that Ponce de Leon never found the Fountain, "for he never sought it in the right place," implying, of course, that it must be found in one's own heart. Hawthorne and O'Connor frequently employ animal or serpent imagery to suggest their estimates of man's nature. The following brief descriptions go beyond the functional and are remarkably similar in their terms and implications:

> A writhing horror twisted itself across his features, like a snake gliding swiftly over them.
>> (Hawthorne's description of Chillingworth,
>> *The Scarlet Letter*, p. 82)

> In the darkness, Mr. Shiftlet's smile stretched like a weary snake waking up by a fire.
>> (Miss O'Connor's description of Shiftlet,
>> "The Life You Save May Be Your Own")

Both writers use the snake in its usual public sense, and both unashamedly use the simile further to remind the reader of the origin of evil and its metaphysical reality. Other direct parallels between

Hawthorne's and Miss O'Connor's stories could be pointed out, but the argument here is not one of direct influence (always difficult to establish) so much as similarity of vision, expressed through content and structure as well as through imagery and symbolism.

It is fortunate that Miss O'Connor's "Mary Ann: The Story of a Little Girl" has finally been collected (*Mystery and Manners*, p. 213), for this short essay illuminates many of the author's attitudes, including her admiration for Hawthorne. The essay serves as the introduction to a "factual account" which she encouraged a group of nuns to write after she had declined to write a book about Mary Ann —a cancer victim who spent her life, from the age of three to twelve, at an Atlanta free cancer home run by the nuns. Half of Mary Ann's face was consumed by a tumor. One eye was removed, but despite the early diagnosis there was no way to save her life. The wonder of it was that Mary Ann lived so long.

When she read the nuns' first letter to her about Mary Ann and examined the photograph they had enclosed, Miss O'Connor's first association—as she writes in her essay—was with Hawthorne's story "The Birthmark." The parallel is obvious, but, as Miss O'Connor writes, "The defect on Mary Ann's cheek could not have been mistaken for a charm. It was plainly grotesque. She belonged to fact and not to fancy" (*Jubilee*, p. 30). From associating and contrasting Mary Ann and Hawthorne's character, Miss O'Connor proceeds to tell the story of her correspondence and meetings with the nuns who wished her to write a book, perhaps a novel, about Mary Ann. In the course of the essay she expresses an incisive appreciation of Hawthorne, whose relevance to her was doubled by virtue of his daughter's being the founder of the order which cared for Mary Ann.

As an artist, Miss O'Connor naturally recoiled from the idea of writing a story about the little girl who had died of cancer. She realized that she would be limited by the facts and that stories about pious children rarely serve to edify. When the nuns accepted her challenge to write their own factual account, Miss O'Connor offered editorial assistance and prepared her introduction. Toward the end of the essay she observed that her reflections about Mary Ann seemed to have little to do with the simplicity and hope of the child's hopeless life. Then she added that Hawthorne could have put her reflections into a fable to "show us what to fear" (*Jubilee*, p. 35).

Useful as Miss O'Connor's critical essays—her first-person talk about fiction writing—are to readers, none reveals so much of her belief as does a single paragraph in "Mary Ann: The Story of a Little Girl." She compacts into that paragraph her concept of good versus evil and her conviction of the palpable reality of evil in our "progressive" society. The paragraph bears her fictional signature, the recurrent image of "unmoored" eyes as suggestive of spiritual, not physical, vision. For all its truth, the paragraph is fiction in that it reveals (as mere statement of fact rarely does) how the writer *sees*: "I later suggested to Sister Evangelist, on an occasion when some of the sisters came down to spend the afternoon with me to discuss the manuscript, that Mary Ann could not have been much *but* good, considering her environment. Sister Evangelist leaned over the arm of her chair and gave me a look. Her eyes were blue and unpredictable behind spectacles that unmoored them slightly. 'We've had some demons!' she said, and a gesture of her hand dismissed my ignorance" (*Jubilee*, p. 35). The paragraph stops short of the abstract statement. It dramatizes: evil is not caused; it is. Rufus Johnson in "The Lame Shall Enter First" is quite right in denying that his crimes result from his clubfoot or from his deprivation, but on that occasion even Flannery O'Connor failed to remember that most basic of her beliefs: evil is not caused; it is.

Having dramatized Sister Evangelist's knowledge, Miss O'Connor assesses in literary and abstract terms the facts of secular society. The statement is applicable to nearly everything she ever wrote; indeed, the burden of her fiction throughout is the message she expressed here in straightforward expository form:

> One of the tendencies of our age is to use the suffering of children to discredit the goodness of God, and once you have discredited His goodness, you are done with Him. The Alymers whom Hawthorne saw as a menace have multiplied. Busy cutting down human imperfection, they are making headway also on the raw material of good. Ivan Karamazov cannot believe as long as one child is in torment; Camus's hero cannot accept the divinity of Christ because of the massacre of the innocents. In this popular pity, we mark our gain in sensibility and loss in vision.
>
> (*Jubilee*, p. 35)

"In *Our Old Home*," writes Miss O'Connor, "Hawthorne tells about a fastidious gentleman who, while going through a Liverpool workhouse, was followed by a wretched and rheumy child, so awful looking that he could not decide what sex it was." The child mutely appealed to be held, and the "fastidious gentleman, after a pause that was significant for himself, picked it up and held it." What Hawthorne does not tell is that he was the fastidious gentleman who, he wrote, "did an heroic act and effected more than he dreamed of toward his final salvation when he took up the loathsome child and caressed it as tenderly as if he had been its father" (*Jubilee*, p. 31).

Hawthorne's daughter, Mother Alphonsa in religious life, later wrote that this account "seemed to her to contain the greatest words her father ever wrote." Speaking of Mother Alphonsa's life of service in cancer hospitals, Miss O'Connor writes: "She discovered much that he sought and fulfilled in a practical way the hidden desires of his life. The ice in the blood which he feared, and which this very fear preserved him from, was turned by her into a warmth which initiated action. If he observed, fearfully but truthfully, if he acted, reluctantly but firmly, she charged ahead, secure in the path his truthfulness had outlined for her" (*Jubilee*, p. 31).

Miss O'Connor's realization about Hawthorne is identical to Marius Bewley's estimate of him as a nonreligious man. Bewley insists that, far from being the convinced, even fanatical, Puritan he has been called, Hawthorne lacked religious conviction almost completely.[9] Nevertheless, Miss O'Connor believes, "Hawthorne gave what he did not have himself," for Mother Alphonsa's work led directly to providing a place in Atlanta for Mary Ann to be cared for; her work, in fulfillment of her father's "hidden desires," made it possible for Mary Ann to learn how to die (*Jubilee*, p. 35).

If Hawthorne's act of caressing the loathsome child in the Liverpool workhouse was the seed from which Mother Alphonsa's life of dedication sprang, then Mary Ann is most certainly the flower of that tree. At any rate, so Flannery O'Connor, herself fated to die early of an incurable disease, interprets the relationship of Hawthorne and Mary Ann: "This action by which charity grows invisibly among us, entwining the living and the dead, is called by the Church the Communion of Saints. It is a communion created upon human imperfection, created from what we make of our grotesque state" (*Jubilee*, p. 35).

There in epigrammatic form is the locale of the eternal crossroads which Hawthorne and Miss O'Connor both sought, in their different ages and in their distinctive ways. Not a denial of charity, not a negation of human love, but a recognition that these virtues serve only to illuminate some parts of the darkness rather than to light the whole—this is the meaning of Flannery O'Connor's insistence upon human imperfection, original sin, and man's grotesque state. Where time, eternity, and place conjoin, there is the communion of saints, and there Miss O'Connor's fanatics, her killers, her demented souls, and her selfish do-gooders rise out of their grotesqueness and converge in their awareness of themselves as sinners in a redeemed world. The message is hope.

Near the end of her life Flannery O'Connor admitted in "The Role of the Catholic Novelist" that she had wasted a great deal of time attempting "to take over the problems" of François Mauriac, but nowhere did she explain the nature of the French Catholic novelist's influence on her. The particular problems she had tried to take over from Mauriac simply were not appropriate to her fiction, for her stories and novels do not deal with the life of sin in such a way as to make it even remotely attractive to her readers. Mauriac's fiction, which frequently actualizes carnal sins, runs the danger of titillating, or tempting, his readers, but even in Miss O'Connor's seduction scenes (in *Wise Blood* and in "Good Country People," for instance) this danger never occurs.

Miss O'Connor's and Mauriac's readers are often disturbed that the stories are not explicit in their religious meanings; neither writer offers spiritual "uplift." The same is true of Nathanael West; for his essentially episodic novels end with failure, not with assurances of the value of the good heart or heavenly bliss. But in these three writers it is nearly always failure which illuminates the possible choices open to man, and there is nearly always a character who needs to profit from definition of those choices. The point leads back to Hawthorne: Miss O'Connor's work affirms that there is always a Mother Alphonsa to "charge ahead, secure in the path of truthfulness" someone else's suffering has outlined.

Eugene E. Murphy said in a lecture at Belmont Abbey College in 1957 that Mauriac "shows the necessity of Grace by illustrating the lamentable and tragic consequences of its absence."[10] Murphy's lecture does not mention Miss O'Connor, but it is true that, like Mauriac, she focuses on a world which seems totally to lack grace. However, neither writer gives us moral fables in which characters do "right" or "wrong" and are to be judged by the ethical standards of Christianity, and neither Mauriac nor O'Connor makes it a practice to deal with Catholics as Catholics.

In his lecture Murphy lists the characters and situations which have come to be regarded as typical of Mauriac; these elements are so recurrent that Mauriac once gave up writing novels, knowing that his books would always be dismissed as "more Mauriac." Among Mauriac's character types is the "duty-doing grandmother," and among the recurrent dramatic situations is the household "sharply divided into enemy camps." *Le Sagouin*, the Mauriac novel which probably influenced Miss O'Connor most deeply, contains both the typical characters and the typical situation. According to Murphy the book's "most unusual feature" is "the choice of a child as the principal personage around whom the drama unfolds" ("The Modern Novel," pp. 21, 22). After 1952 the dutiful grandmother, the divided household and the divided family, and children as central personages recur often in Miss O'Connor's works. (Although she had published her first story in 1946 and her first novel in 1952, such trademarks do not appear until "A Good Man Is Hard to Find," the first distinctively O'Connor story, published in 1953.)

Of the materials probably suggested to Miss O'Connor by Mauriac's *The Weakling*, the most important are the idea of sacramental drowning, the use of a secularist schoolteacher, and the symbolic use of a dark line of trees. The drowning of the neglected child Harry Ashfield concludes "The River" (1953), and the drowning of Mr. Fortune concludes "A View of the Woods" (1957). In *The Violent Bear It Away* the relationships among Rayber, his idiot son Bishop, and Francis Marion Tarwater are essentially the same as those of Sheppard, his dull son Norton, and Rufus Johnson in "The Lame Shall Enter First"; these relationships are similar to those of Robert Bordas, his bright son Jean-Pierre, and Guillaume de Cernès, *le sagouin* of Mauriac's 1952 novel. In Mauriac's book Bordas's refusal to teach Guillaume leads to the boy's drowning; in Miss O'Connor's novel both Rayber and young Tarwater are responsible for Bishop's death by water, and in "The Lame Shall Enter First" Norton hangs himself after learning from the seemingly malevolent Johnson that he may rejoin his mother in heaven, "where spaceships can't go," if he dies without sin. In Miss O'Connor's story, as in Mauriac's, a school-teacher, morally responsible for a child's death, is altered spiritually as a result of that death. Despite some apparent differences, it would not be extravagant to say that Robert Bordas is the model both for Rayber and for Sheppard; furthermore, the circumstances and motives of the double tragedy of Galéas de Cernès and his son Guillaume provide recurrent elements in Miss O'Connor's fiction, including the dragon or monster theme which recurs in all her stories about drowning. Mauriac's father and son go into the river to escape their wife and mother, who is identified with the Gorgon—thematically similar to Miss O'Connor's recurrent "dragon of secularism."

The similarities between Mauriac's novel and Miss O'Connor's subsequent work notwithstanding, one must insist that the differences in their individual gifts preclude the possibility of imitation. Though Miss O'Connor clearly employs materials suggested by *The Weakling*, she transcends her source. However, just as Mauriac treats his people of southwestern France in such a way as to invest their lives with universal importance, so Miss O'Connor renders her Georgians in cosmic portraits, unrestricted either by regional or by literary influences. An important comment appears at the end of *The Enemy* (*Le Mal*), published in the same volume as *The Weakling*. Mauriac writes: "The real story of Fabien Dézaymeries should, properly speaking, begin at this point, for all that had gone before was in the nature of a prologue. But how is one to describe the secret drama of a man who struggles to subdue his earthly heritage, that drama which finds expression neither in words nor gestures? Where is the artist who may dare to imagine the processes and shifts of the great protagonist—Grace? It is the mark of our slavery and of our wretchedness that we can, without lying, paint a faithful portrait only of the passions."[11] Mauriac's method, here observed in the story itself, is Miss O'Connor's method also. For instance, in "The Comforts of Home" (a story that appeared in the *Kenyon Review* in 1960), she leaves Thomas stripped of his defenses. A murderer whose efforts to frame a "moral moron" have backfired and rendered him vulnerable to the scorn he has heaped on his intended victim, Thomas is in the defenseless position in which the "processes and shifts of the great protagonist—Grace" may affect him, but Miss O'Connor ends the story with this prologue.

The Weakling, another prologue, is short, like Miss O'Connor's novels. Robert Bordas is prepared for spiritual self-realization by his failure to meet his obligation to the human spirit slumbering in the miserable body of Guillaume de Cernès. The French title, *Le Sagouin,* designates an animal, a squirrel monkey; as Murphy wrote, when applied to humans it denotes slovenliness ("The Modern Novel," p. 20). *Le Sagouin,* Guillaume, is the only child of Paule and baron Galéas de Cernès. Paule's marriage to Galéas resulted from her desire for a title, but she is thwarted in this desire by the longevity of Galéas's mother, *madame la baronne.* Only once have Galéas and Paule slept together; Guillaume is the result. Almost an exact replica of his father, he calls to mind the physical similarities between children and adults in several of Miss O'Connor's stories. (Bishop in *The Violent Bear It Away* looks like old Mason Tarwater, Mary Fortune Pitts in "A View of the Woods" looks like her grandfather, and Nelson in "The Artificial Nigger" looks like Mr. Head.)

In Mauriac's story Guillaume, after a single lesson from the schoolmaster, Bordas, is told he cannot return. Bordas, who fears involvement with Paule and possible scandal, hides behind his supposed communist commitment as his reason for not teaching Guillaume. The child and his father leave their home, where Paule and the aged baroness are quarreling, and go to the graveyard and eventually to the river where they drown. The official view is that Galéas drowned trying to save his son, but there are hints that father and son drowned themselves to escape the woman with the Gorgon's face "blotched with bilious yellow"—the sex-starved, drunken Paule (p. 72).

The tragedy, if one may call it that, is not dramatized in the story; the father and son reach the riverbank lined with great trees, and after a paragraph about the trees, one learns of the events after the bodies are recovered. The grief-stricken Austrian nurse disapproves of what she takes to be the baroness's relief at the deaths of her incompetent son and grandson. Paule returns to her uncle and aunt only to be hospitalized with a malignant tumor. Glad of her approaching death, she fears no judgment, for she "was absolved in her own sight from the horror she had felt for a son who was the image of a hated father." Furthermore, "she had spewed up the Cernès family, because nausea is something that one cannot control." By the end of the novel, however, Paule regards herself as guilty of a crime "for which there was no pardon," and with her failure to distinguish night from day, there seems to be hope even for her: "Pain knocked at the door; pain entered in and took its lodgement, and started slowly to eat her life away" (pp. 75–76).

All that remains is a last look at the schoolteacher. Though he and his wife Léone have avoided discussing it, they know why *le sagouin* died. Bordas's appearance (he is unshaven and improperly clad) suggests that his values have been altered; he wanders into Jean-Pierre's room and takes up the *Mysterious Island,* the book from which Guillaume had read during his only lesson: "The book opened of itself. '. . . The poor wretch was about to plunge into the creek which lay between him and the forest. For a brief moment, his legs were like two springs at the moment of release. . . . But almost at once he fell back, half collapsing, and a large tear welled up in his eye. "Ah," exclaimed Cyril Smith: "if you can cry, it means you have once more become a man!" ' " (p. 77). The passage is the one Guillaume had read; it is ironically appropriate now, and Bordas, realizing the extent of his guilt in not helping the boy, vows that for Guillaume's sake he will never again refuse to "give of his utmost to those who came to him." But of course it is too late for *le sagouin,* whose awakening might have been the task for which Robert Bordas had been born. The teacher recalls that he had sent the boy into darkness; then he wonders if it was really darkness: "He strained his eyes in an effort to see beyond material things, beyond the walls and the furniture of this, his house, beyond the tiled roof, beyond the star-pointed night, beyond the winter constellations. He sat there, seeking the kingdom of the spirit where, rapt away into eternity, the boy could see him still, and on his cheek, stubbly with unshaven beard, a tear he had not thought to wipe away" (p. 78).

Mauriac's focus on the schoolteacher—his materialistic values and his dedication to the class war which he thinks can alter human society but which he uses to excuse himself from real human involvement—concludes with Bordas's self-realization, which necessarily requires a quest for values beyond material ones. His tear may suggest the attainment of a new kind of manhood, but his most important gain in the story is awareness of his own inadequacy and of the reality of the "kingdom of the spirit," which he had hitherto denied.

Though Mauriac does not say so, *The Weakling,* like *The Enemy,* is but a prologue: the real struggle begins after the story ends. However, Mauriac's last paragraph suggests the nature of this struggle and the import of the deaths of the Cernès father and son: "the spring grass strayed into the churchyard," roots "took hold upon the untended graves," and moss obliterated the epitaphs.

A year after Mauriac's book appeared in America, Miss O'Connor published five of her best stories, including "The River," in which a miserably neglected child walks into a river thinking it will take him to "the Kingdom of Christ." In another of that year's stories, the justly famous "A Good Man Is Hard to Find," she introduced the dark line of trees, her recurrent emblem foreshadowing death and revelation. Probably taking her cue from Mauriac's use of the Gorgon, Miss O'Connor also began developing the "dragon of secularism," or the monster, the meaning of which had been implicit in *Wise Blood.* The epigraph for *A Good Man Is Hard to Find* serves to alert the reader to her emphasis; at the same time it identifies unifying features of the collection: in one sense *A Good Man Is Hard to Find* is a book of the road, a collection of stories about people on the go. This is clear from the epigraph:

> The Dragon is by the side of the road, watching those who pass. Beware lest he devour you. We go to the Father of Souls, but it is necessary to pass by the Dragon.
>
> St. Cyril of Jerusalem

Miss O'Connor had established the same central image in *Wise Blood,* which emphasizes Haze Motes's dependence upon his rat-colored Essex automobile. Because his faith in his car, the dragon, is unshakable, it stands in the way of his seeing spiritual truth. Therefore the destruction of the car leads to his (and Mrs. Flood's) salvation.

In "The River" Miss O'Connor names her monster, or dragon, and again associates him with the automobile. Old Mr. Paradise, a scoffer who is said to look like a hog and then like an "ancient water monster," is first seen sitting on the bumper of his car at a faith-healing meeting. Later the child Harry Ashfield walks into the river, hoping to be swept away to the Kingdom of Christ, as the young preacher Bevel Summers had promised, but the river will not take him. Mr.

Paradise's shout and his piglike appearance drive the boy farther into the water; after Harry has been swept away, Mr. Paradise, who had failed to "save" the boy, occasionally surfaced in the water "like some ancient water monster and stood empty-handed, staring with his dull eyes as far down the river line as he could see."

The monster recurs in "A View of the Woods," a story in the final collection, which brings together death by drowning, the monster, the dark line of trees, and the woods. After a terrible struggle in the woods with his granddaughter, ending in his accidentally killing her to "teach her a lesson," old Mr. Fortune runs into the lake to his death: he sees "on both sides of him . . . that the gaunt trees had thickened into mysterious dark files that were marching across the water and away into the darkness," but when he looks for someone to help him, he sees only a "huge yellow monster gorging itself on clay." The significance of the trees and of the bulldozer increases steadily from the title and the first paragraph to the end.

Miss O'Connor frequently associates the dark line of trees with the Catholic sacraments and with motion (one of her favorite themes), especially with highways. In "A View of the Woods," she associates the trees with the mystery of Christ's suffering, with death, and with baptism. In "A Temple of the Holy Ghost," included in her first collection, she associates the dark woods with blood; the image is the sun as "an elevated Host drenched in blood," which leaves a line in the sky "like a red clay road hanging over the trees." Liturgically, then, "A Temple of the Holy Ghost" is associated with the Eucharist, and "A View of the Woods" with baptism. On other occasions she uses the dark wall of trees ironically. In *The Violent Bear It Away* the trees listen while a traveling salesman, speeding forward "on the black untwisting highway," subverts the message of love: he tells young Tarwater "that you couldn't sell a copper flue to a man you didn't love."

The emphasis on the woods as a place of revelation does not occur in any of Miss O'Connor's stories prior to "A Good Man Is Hard to Find"; in that story the Misfit, a psychopathic killer, sends the members of the Bailey family into the nearby woods to die at the hands of his henchmen. The scene of the family's automobile accident which puts them in the Misfit's power is dominated by the trees; on all sides of them are "more woods tall and dark and deep." Just before her death the grandmother realizes that there was "nothing around her but woods."

In *The Weakling* Mauriac associates the presence of the trees with the deaths of Galéas and Guillaume. At first the father "could not bring himself to face the issue to which these last two of the Cernès line were hastening." Then, "A tremble of alder leaves spoke of the nearby river. Not now was it the King of the Alders who, in a final gallop, was pursuing the boy, but the boy now who was leading his uncrowned and insulted father toward the sleeping waters of the weir. . . . They were close now to the watery confines of that kingdom where never more would they be harassed by wife or mother. They would be delivered from the Gorgon; they would sleep" (p. 73). Here the similarity of Galéas's pursuit of Guillaume to Rayber's following Tarwater should be observed. Later Rayber dreams that he is pursuing the boy until the trail turns and the boy is pursuing him. Furthermore, though Tarwater actually drowns Bishop, Rayber has made it necessary for him to do so; finally, Rayber profits from Bishop's drowning in much the same way that Robert Bordas benefits from Guillaume's death.

Reaching the shade of the tall pines on the riverbank, Galéas loses sight of his son; there is no one else about, and "every witness had withdrawn from this small corner of the world that the act might be accomplished which these two were fated to perform—one leading the other? or urging him forward unwillingly?—who would ever know?" Just as we do not witness the drowning of Bishop in *The Violent Bear It Away,* so we do not see the death of Galéas and his son. At the height of our interest in the act they were fated to perform, our attention is distracted from Galéas and Guillaume and focused instead on the "giant pines crowding about the weir." "They burned during the following August, left too long untapped. For a long while they spread their calcined limbs above the sleeping water; for a long time they reared against the sky their blackened faces" (p. 74).

Although the burning of the trees is an event of the future, Mauriac projects it into the action of the present, effectively halting that action. In a sense the drownings occur during the interruption, for when the narrator turns back to Galéas and Guillaume, he says, "The accepted view was that Galéas had jumped into the water to save his son" (p. 74). Part of this narrative technique finds its way into *The Violent Bear It Away*: Rayber knows what is happening on the lake and what will happen after the drowning even before it happens, but the reader does not get an account of what happened until the following section, where, appropriately, Miss O'Connor again introduces her monster in close proximity to Bishop's drowning. Both writers withhold their most intensely dramatic action to be narrated after the fact.

To escape the Gorgon, Mauriac's characters enter the shade of the pine trees, the symbolic importance of which is greatly magnified by the report of their burning—almost as if of their own power and volition. Here one recalls Tarwater's burning the woods in Miss O'Connor's novel.

Though Mauriac's symbolic use of the pines is closely related to the waste of human lives through devotion to petty aims and through lack of human love, as exemplified in his chief characters, the symbolism also extends to the whole community and to the church itself. The unused church, the unconsecrated family chapel, the unkept graveyard, and the untapped pine trees represent human failures to take advantage of spiritual power. Class snobbery, sexual and moral prohibitions, reliance on theoretical communism, and dependence on middle-class values prevent the tapping of spiritual resources. Bordas finally seeks to see beyond the material and into the spiritual, but he does so too late to help the miserable members of the Cernès family.

In the novel's world of waste and hatred, Guillaume provides the most positive hope: "What was that word his mother had used just now? . . . He tried to remember, and could think only of 'regenerate'" (p. 71). Like Miss O'Connor's Harry Ashfield ("The River"), Norton ("The Lame Shall Enter First"), and Bishop (*The Violent Bear It Away*), Guillaume is a holy innocent; his salvation is sure. These holy innocents complete triangles in Miss O'Connor's stories just as Guillaume completes the triangle composed of Bordas, Jean-Pierre, and Guillaume. Deifying intelligence and its secular application, Bordas idolizes his son; Rayber places his hope in educating Francis Marion Tarwater; and Sheppard takes in the high-IQ Rufus Johnson, whom he woos intellectually at the expense of his own son. But in each instance the death of a child, to use the words spoken by the prophet Mason Tarwater in *The Violent Bear It Away*, "burns clean the eyes" of a secular, materialist adult. In "The River" Mr. Paradise looks as far as he can see with his "dull eyes" down the shoreline; in *The Violent Bear It Away* Rayber collapses when he realizes that the pain for which he has been waiting, so he can deny it, will not come; and in "The Lame Shall Enter First" Sheppard "reeled back like a man on the edge of a pit" when he saw Norton's body hanging from the beam from which "he had launched his flight into space."

As Professor Murphy says of Mauriac, "when this French novelist leaves his creatures, they're looking into their hearts and souls, they are ready for Grace" ("The Modern Novel," p. 24). Neither Mauriac nor Flannery O'Connor abandons hope; both recognize the world as redeemed, and their "prologues" dramatize the potential of grace. Both are capable of providing their secular readers with "desperate answers," but both have testified to the real existence of the eternal crossroads. Both writers, if asked to localize the crossroads, would doubtless have placed it near the woods, recalling Christ's sacrifice and the lack of love which permits lives, like untapped pines, to burn themselves black.

CHAPTER THREE

'Wise Blood' & What Came Before

WISE BLOOD, Flannery O'Connor's first novel, may owe part of its excellence to nine pages of comments sent her by Caroline Gordon, who read the first revision of the book. Robert Giroux had accepted the first draft for publication by Harcourt, Brace, and Miss O'Connor asked her friend Robert Fitzgerald to send the revision to Caroline Gordon. She later asked if Miss Gordon would read the second revision. As Fitzgerald notes in his introduction to *Everything That Rises Must Converge,* Miss O'Connor acknowledged that Miss Gordon's comments "certainly increased my education. . . . All the changes are efforts after what she suggested in that letter and I am much obliged to her."[1] Several questions come to mind here: had Miss O'Connor previously altered the several chapters which had already been published as stories in various periodicals, or was Miss Gordon partly responsible for those alterations? Important though they are, the alterations of the stories are infrequent enough to suggest that Miss Gordon must have made other suggestions. Fitzgerald's introduction to *Everything That Rises* records only one such suggestion: he comments that Miss Gordon thought the style of the "narrator should be more consistently distinct from the style of the characters" (p. xviii).

As recently as 1965, Walter Sullivan complained that the theme of *Wise Blood* "dribbled" out of the loosely constructed novel.[2] Two years earlier Melvin J. Friedman had called the novel "episodic and fragmentary," saying that it was comprised of "short stories strung together to form a novel."[3] The fault here is the critics', not Miss O'Connor's, for her first novel is a skillfully crafted work of prose fiction. It depends on the same reversal technique to be found in her later novel, which, ironically, is generally praised as being better structured than *Wise Blood.* Friedman's comment about "short stories strung together to form a novel" would never have appeared in print had he compared the stories as they appeared in periodicals and the chapters as they function in the novel. For the stories and the chapters derived from them are not identical.

Before examining the changes in the stories incorporated in *Wise Blood,* it would be well to identify the other stories published before 1952. There were but three of them; two were later revised and re-titled for inclusion in the two collections. "The Geranium," rewritten as "Judgement Day," appears in *Everything That Rises Must Converge;* the original and revised forms of this story will be examined in chapter six. "The Woman on the Stairs," retitled "A Stroke of Good Fortune," is included in *A Good Man Is Hard to Find;* the two forms of this story will be examined in chapter four. There remains but one early story to be considered here, "The Capture," which Miss O'Connor neither collected nor revised after its appearance in *Mademoiselle* in November 1948. Of her work published before her death, "The Capture" is one of two stories which remain uncollected; the other is "The Partridge Festival," originally intended for inclusion in the last collection but withdrawn in favor of "Parker's Back." This story and the probable reasons for its withdrawal will also be considered in chapter six.

"The Capture" is about an eleven-year-old boy who chases a wounded turkey into the woods and, after cursing and renouncing God because he cannot catch the turkey, finds it lying dead in his path. He decides to abjure cursing and the wicked life he had intended to lead and proudly sets off for home and the anticipated admiration of his family. He hopes God will give him something to do to show his gratitude; specifically, he hopes to see a beggar so he can give away the dime he has in his pocket. Along the way he revels in the townspeople's interest in his turkey, and to his joy he does see a beggar (albeit one rumored to be rich) on whom he thrusts his dime. He magnanimously shows his turkey to some country children who have followed him; they steal the bird, leaving the boy shocked and wordless. First he creeps, then runs homeward; as he runs he is certain that "Something Awful was tearing after him with its arms rigid and its fingers ready to clutch." The pursuer has become the pursued.

The story is but slightly more complicated than the plot summary indicates. The boy Ruller lives in a divided household; his parents and his grandmother are worried about his older brother, Hane, who has taken up pool playing and cigarette smoking. Ruller's desire to curse and "shock the pants off his grandmother" results from the wish to be unusual, the same wish which makes him try so hard to catch the turkey. An unusual feature of the story, one that Miss O'Connor was to use far more effectively in *The Violent Bear It Away*, is the abstraction of the boy into two parts—one which speaks and one which listens. As he practices cursing, he is shocked to realize "he'd never heard himself think in that tone before." In *The Violent Bear It Away* young Tarwater has a similar response to his inner voice, which later becomes his "friend."

A defect of the story is the enormity of that "Something Awful" which pursues Ruller home, an enormity for which the reader is not fully prepared. The boy's play—he pretends to be a sheriff pursuing a band of rustlers—is thoroughly childlike; his renunciation of God and his unabashed "swap" with God are amusing, and, though the reader believes in the boy, he cannot go very deeply into his mind. Ruller's flight from "Something Awful" remains childish in its context; it cannot be reconciled with the suspicion that Miss O'Connor's conclusion was intended to achieve greater significance.

In *Wise Blood* she realizes that greater significance. In particular, the alterations in "The Train," *Sewanee Review* (April 1948), to make it suitable as chapter one of *Wise Blood* reveal either that Miss O'Connor had been working on a novel all along, or that she knew her craft well enough to avoid "stringing short stories together." Major symbols of the novel did not appear in "The Train" as it was originally published but were added as a part of the novel's total design. Three other stories, "The Heart of the Park," "The Peeler," and "Enoch and the Gorilla," required less revision, but the third story posed special problems of transition since Haze Motes does not appear in the short-story version at all. These four revised stories constitute more than four chapters of the finished novel; "Enoch and the Gorilla" serves as the basis for chapters eleven and twelve, while the other stories, with transitional material added, represent a chapter each.

In the original version of "The Train" the central character's name is Hazel Wicker, a name less satisfactory than Hazel Motes, who became the novel's central character. However, the diminutive, Haze, functions well either with Wicker or with Motes, for both names are associated with vision: a *wick* provides light, and *motes* suggests the biblical beams and motes obstructing true vision. "The Train" reveals Haze's thoughts about the Negro porter to whom he wishes to speak. Haze is convinced that the porter is Cash Simmons's son who ran away from the South. In another of her early stories, "The Geranium," a white man assumes that a Negro he sees in New York is really a southern Negro; the revision of this story, "Judgement Day," develops the theme of identity even further. In "The Train" Haze, on his way to Chattanooga, recalls that he was "supposed to go to his sister's in Taulkinham on his last furlough when he came up from the camp in Georgia." Similarly, Ruby Hill in "A Stroke of Good Fortune" lives in the city and has bought collard greens to cook for her brother who is on furlough. Thus it appears that as early as her second published short story, Miss O'Connor had begun to create a cast of fully realized characters from whom she could choose to fill a minor role in a story.

In "The Train" Haze talks to Mrs. Wallace Ben Hosen, who had been Miss Hitchcock before she married; in *Wise Blood* he talks to Mrs. Hitchcock, who had been Miss Weatherman before she married. The alteration of the story, in light of this conversation, provides part of the significance of Mrs. Flood's name at the end of the novel. To Mrs. Hosen's question "Are you going home?" Haze replies that he is "getting off at Chattanooga"; in the novel he simply says, "No, I'm not." Mrs. Hitchcock's similar question is answered metaphorically at the end of the novel when Mrs. Flood speaks to Haze's dead body: "I see you've come home." Mrs. Hitchcock had said, "I see you're going home."

In the novel Mrs. Hitchcock admits she's not going home, either, but to Florida to visit her daughter; she confides that her grandchildren call her "Mammadoll." The short story does not contain Haze's belligerent assertion to Mrs. Hitchcock in the novel: "I reckon you think you been redeemed." The novel juxtaposes this assertion with his remarks about the porter, who "was raised in the same place I was raised but says he's from Chicago." Haze is doubtless aware that Mrs. Hitchcock and the Eastrod Negro who claims to be from Chicago have something in common.

The scene in the diner where Haze waits in line to eat is repeated in the novel, as is the fact that he thinks of his mother after he gets into his berth. He recalls that he has slept in his family's empty house, where nothing remains but his mother's "shiffer-robe." The story does not mention that Haze has his mother's silver-rimmed glasses, which he sometimes wears to hurt his eyes, nor does it include his dream about his grandfather. The story ends when Haze wakes, looks out of the berth, sees the porter at the opposite end of the car, and falls back sick. He says nothing in the story, whereas the first chapter in the novel ends with the porter's "sour triumphant" observation that "Jesus been a long time gone," in response to Haze's obviously profane use of Jesus' name. Haze's desire to get out of the berth is caused by his recalling his mother in her casket. Later in the novel one learns that his first self-imposed penance came after he had seen a naked woman in a casket at a carnival sideshow; seeing his mother afterward, he had put rocks in his shoes and walked on them.

The statement "I reckon you think you been redeemed" is the first clue in the novel that Haze is "Jesus hungry," and his calling on Jesus at the end of the chapter reinforces the clue. The porter, pretending to be something he is not, represents secular society, which does not move to help anyone but triumphs in its awareness that "Jesus been a long time gone." Like the caged animals which recur in the novel, Haze is enclosed in the berth and in the train; finally, he will realize that he is caged in his body and by his senses.

Chapter five of *Wise Blood* was originally published in 1949 as "The Heart of the Park." By then Miss O'Connor had changed Hazel Wicker's name again, this time to Hazel Weaver, and had created her memorable characters Sabbath Lily and Asa Hawks but had named them Sabbath and Asa Moats, a suitable last name since it signifies both a visual obstruction and a protective body of water. Finally, she recognized the suitability of Motes as Haze's last name and Hawks as Asa and Sabbath's last name, and she invented the ironic second name Lily for Sabbath.

Though the changes in "The Heart of the Park" are fewer than those in "The Train," some of them are quite important. Some appear to be stylistic but are in fact more nearly structural, as, for instance, in the refreshment stand scene. Enoch Emery's "ritual," which concludes with his visit to the mummy at the "dark secret center of the park," begins with refreshments. In "The Heart of the Park" Haze looks at the waitress as if "he were looking at a piece of wood," but in the novel he looks at her as if "he were looking at a wall." This change supports the confinement theme basic to the novel's meaning and already suggested in Haze's desire to get out of the berth; it relates to a complex web of images: the train, berth, caskets, "shiffer-robe," animal cages, and mummy case. Haze's statement in the story, "I AIN'T clean," had to be changed to "I AM clean" in the novel. The final sentence in "The Heart of the Park" reiterates the beating of Enoch Emery's "secret blood" "in the center of the city." In the novel Miss O'Connor added: "Then he knew that whatever was expected of him was only just beginning." This addition renders the bizarre events of the story functional in the novel, for Enoch's ritual in the park and his wise blood's response to Haze lead finally to his encaging himself in the van, overpowering the man in the gorilla suit, and stealing the suit. Likewise, his blood tells him to steal the mummy and give it to Haze.

By the time "The Peeler" appeared in print (1949), Miss O'Connor had settled on Hazel Motes as her character's name. "The Peeler" became chapter three of the novel; it introduces Haze and Enoch to one another and fortifies the alienation theme, particularly through Enoch's pathetic quest for friendship. Haze responds as coldly to Enoch as the Negro porter had responded to Haze. In the story Miss O'Connor does not include the lion on which Enoch sits outside the auditorium as he and Haze listen to Asa Hawks preach. The biblical relevance of lions in *The Violent Bear It Away* suggests that the addition of the lion has symbolic importance: in *The Violent Bear It Away* the false prophet is to beware of the Lord's lion; in *Wise Blood* Enoch's fleshly and materialistic orientation makes him a danger to Haze. More important, Miss O'Connor changed Haze and Enoch's conversation. In *Wise Blood* Enoch tells Haze, "You ain't got no woman nor nothing to do. I knew when I first seen you you didn't have nobody nor nothing but Jesus." "The Peeler" lacks the important words "but Jesus." Similarly, in the story Enoch does not say, "You act like you think you got wiser blood than anybody else, but you ain't! I'm the one has it. Not you." This claim, added to the novel, makes explicit the difference between the Jesus-hungry Haze and the woman-hungry Enoch. Haze is impeded by spiritual rather than physiological needs, but Enoch—even in his gorilla suit—still seeks to fill the physical gap in his life by extending his hands to the frightened lovers.

"Enoch and the Gorilla" appeared in 1952 just before the novel's publication. The story deals wholly with Enoch, but in the novel Enoch's activities are interwoven with Haze's preaching of the Church Without Jesus. The spectacles, which Miss O'Connor had added to chapter one, recur here when Haze casts them aside with the mummy. Chapter twelve of the novel is largely the same as the latter half of the original story.

These comparisons—in addition to their value as indications of Miss O'Connor's method of creation in the careful addition of important elements to the novel—also indicate the significance of the novel's reversal technique and its contrapuntal treatment of Haze and Enoch. Far from being left unfinished (as some critics charge), Enoch's story informs Haze's story; both young men make a choice but they are prompted by different forces. Not wise blood like Enoch's but rather the realization of the meaning of sin and the possibility of redemption renders Haze Motes (alias Hazel Wicker, alias Hazel Weaver) a Christian in spite of himself. He is the prototype of the primitive believer set free from the physical, utopian dreams of the secular city. Miss O'Connor asserts that not a return to the animal but an overcoming of the animal will permit man at last to come home.

Although Miss O'Connor did not provide formal divisions in *Wise Blood,* the relationships among parts are largely the same as in the formally imposed structure of *The Violent Bear It Away.* The organization of both books emphasizes the reiterated symbols through which she creates her "true country," in which all action is significant action and characters assume prophetic, not merely naturalistic, reality.

Wise Blood contains fourteen chapters which break into three separate parts, with the central four chapters (six through nine) providing the content on which depends the ultimate reversal of the quest which is the action proper of the book. Thus part one (chapters one through five) balances part three (chapters ten through fourteen), while part two spans the longer units. If one imagines the novel as an arch structure, part one leads to the apex of part two, and part

three provides the reversal of part one. This reversal provides fulfillment of the quest inherent in all the action and symbols, an assertion
which will be supported by examining the novel's opening and closing sequences.

In the opening sequence on the train Haze Motes is wearing a
new "glaring blue" suit and is sitting opposite Mrs. Hitchcock, who
says, "I guess you're going home." She leans forward, "squinting at his
eyes, trying almost to look into them." They seem to her like "passages leading somewhere," and she notices that the "outline of a skull
under his skin was plain and insistent."[4] On the last page of the novel
Miss O'Connor repeats this sentence but omits the word *insistent*.
Haze, his blue suit now faded, lies dead. Mrs. Flood says, "I see
you've come home" and grabs his hands while she observes his face:
"The outline of a skull was plain under his skin and the deep burned
eye sockets seemed to lead into the dark tunnel where he had disappeared. She leaned closer and closer to his face, looking deep into
them. . . . She shut her eyes and saw the pin point of light. . . .
She sat staring with her eyes shut into his eyes, and felt as if she had
finally got to the beginning of something she couldn't begin, and she
saw him moving farther and farther away, farther and farther into
darkness until he was the pin point of light" (p. 126). Haze's quest,
which has passed from denial and repudiation to ritualistic cleansing,
has brought him home, and his coming home serves as a light, albeit
a pinpoint of light, for his landlady. The woman on the train (Mrs.
Hitchcock) and the landlady (Mrs. Flood) are similar, both genteel
and respectable, and through both of them Miss O'Connor establishes
the significance of Haze Motes's eyes.

The importance of vision is also indicated by Miss O'Connor's care
in selecting her protagonist's name. Her final choice of Haze Motes
embodies the ironic reversal of the first and last pages. Since *haze*
used as a noun means "vagueness of mind or mental perception," the
verb *to haze* suggests "making vague or obscure." The verb also carries an initiatory or punitive meaning, as in schoolboy hazing of a
newcomer. In its primary sense *motes* means "small particles," thus
relating to the pinpoint of light Haze becomes at the end; Mrs. Flood
calls him "Mr. Motes" before looking into his eyes. For most readers
motes suggests another meaning, the scriptural motes and beams,
obstructions to vision.

Haze wears his mother's silver-rimmed spectacles to hurt his eyes. He desires physical mortification, but he also desires a special sort of vision. In his dream of his mother's return from the grave "with that look on her face, unrested and looking," one is aware that she is looking for something discernible not to the physical but to the spiritual eye. "In the dream, Haze had seen the shadow that came down over her face and pulled her mouth down as if she wasn't any more satisfied dead than alive, as if she were going to spring up and shove the lid back and fly out to satisfy herself" (p. 19). At the moment in the novel's action when Haze rejects the "new jesus," the mummy Enoch has stolen for him, he is wearing his mother's spectacles, which he then throws away. After these symbolic acts he leaves Sabbath Lily and pursues his course toward the ultimate self-mortification of blinding himself. In the beginning Haze has eyes and sees not; in the end he is blinded but sees. Simultaneous rejection of spectacles, mummy, and physical lust (Sabbath) is part of the progression to true sight. The secret of the book clearly rests in the meaning and nature of vision.

Wise Blood is a book about a Christian *malgré lui*. (For Miss O'Connor's understanding of this term, see her 1962 note to the Signet edition, 3 *by Flannery O'Connor*.) Appropriately, the sacrament of baptism is important in *Wise Blood*, though it is treated implicitly and allusively rather than being the central act as it is in Miss O'Connor's second novel, *The Violent Bear It Away*. Haze's landlady's name, Mrs. Flood, is important in this use of baptism: *flood* combines the destructive and regenerative implications of water. Jehovah sent the flood both to destroy the world's people and to reaffirm truth. Mrs. Flood is partly responsible for Haze's death. Nevertheless, he says to the police she has sent to bring him home, "I want to go on where I'm going," and his death is a victory that serves as Mrs. Flood's pinpoint of light. Traditionally, baptism has been regarded as a death to sin and a rebirth in Christ; it is an outward sign of an inner grace.

Specific details and a direct literary allusion indicate the importance of baptism in *Wise Blood*. Near the turning point of the book, Sabbath Lily's landlady "was out on the porch looking distrustfully into the storm," but "Haze Motes didn't notice the rain, only [his] car; if asked he would not have been able to say that it was raining."

Mrs. Flood "was not religious or morbid, for which every day she thanked her stars"; her distrust of the storm, however, reveals her true character, just as Haze's lack of awareness of the rain reveals his. Later, when Haze opens a door to throw out the "new jesus," drops of rain "hung sparkling from the brim of his hat"; the rain had fallen "on his hat with loud splatters as if it were falling on tin," and with the first contact with the rain, he had "jumped back and stood with a cautious look, as if he were bracing himself for a blow." Baptism has occurred symbolically, though Haze is not yet fully prepared to accept the truth he has seen in the shriveled mummy. Preparation for the baptismal scene occurs in chapter five.

Through allusion to part four of Eliot's *The Waste Land* ("Death by Water") Miss O'Connor heightens the reader's awareness of the double function of water. The allusion serves also to establish the book's mythic implications by bringing to mind the poem's central consciousness, Tiresias, "throbbing between two lives"; for Tiresias is a blind seer, whose power of prophecy compensates for his loss of physical sight. *Wise Blood*'s reversal techniques as well as much of its specific content bring to mind also Oedipus, who blinded himself in expiation of carnal sins and spiritual blindness. In *Oedipus Rex* Oedipus's father, wishing to avert death at his son's hands, sets in motion the events which will make that death inevitable; similarly, Haze Motes's efforts to repudiate lead finally to acceptance. Oedipus, living in a foreign kingdom, hears the prophecy that he will kill his father, and in fleeing his foster father's kingdom to avoid the crime foretold, he rushes toward the crossroads where he will meet and kill his real father. Further, once Oedipus begins to seek the truth, he persists, little suspecting the implications of what he will discover. Eventually, both Oedipus and Haze discover a truth unlike any they had expected, and both seek inward sight through loss of external sight.

The truth begins to dawn for Haze in his two terrible confrontations with the "new jesus," which Enoch Emery shows him and later steals for him and which Sabbath Lily claims as her own. Showing Haze the mummy in its museum case, Enoch says "in a church whisper . . . 'it says he was once as tall as you or me' " (p. 57). Part four of *The Waste Land* concludes with these words:

Gentile or Jew
O you who turn the wheel and look to windward,
Consider Phlebas, who was once handsome and tall as you.

This shortest section of Eliot's poem is a turning point, for in it Eliot negates the phony clairvoyante Madame Sosostoris's earlier warning to fear death by water and suggests the regenerative powers of water. In part two (ll. 47–48) Eliot had associated Phlebas with Shakespeare's Ferdinand in *The Tempest* ("Those are pearls that were his eyes"); in parts one (l. 52) and two (l. 209) he associates Phlebas with Eugenides, possibly a pervert and certainly obsessed with profits. By part four, the sea-change has worked its magic; Phlebas has forgotten "the profit and loss":

A current under sea
Picked his bones in whispers. As he rose and fell
He passed the stages of his age and youth
Entering the whirlpool.

Phlebas is a "sign" to Gentile and Jew; he has passed the stages of life and has entered the whirlpool, just as Miss O'Connor's characters must pass the dragon, overcome the purely material, to achieve revelation.

Enoch Emery's "church whisper" expresses his awe in the face of the inexplicable—Eliot's sea-change and Miss O'Connor's "diminishment," which are both ways of saying death. His response is appropriately physical, but the passage climaxes a series of coffin images and contains promises of things to come. Staring into the mummy's case, Haze sees his face reflected; a woman and her two children come in, and "the reflection of her face appeared grinning on the glass, over Haze Motes's." Haze's neck jerked back "and he made a noise. It might have come from the man inside the case. In a second Enoch knew it had" (p. 57). Haze is thus identified with the mummy, and, by extension, with Phlebas. Haze flees, and when Enoch pursues him, he stones the boy.

Both Enoch and Sabbath accept the "new jesus," which fills needs in their starved lives, but in Haze the mummy serves to prompt spiritual awareness. Sabbath receives the mummy from Enoch, bears it into Haze's room, and demands, "Call me momma now." At the end of chapter two the whore Mrs. Watts had told him, "That's okay, son, Momma don't mind if you ain't a preacher." On his second night with Mrs. Watts, Haze recalls a sideshow at a carnival where he had seen a naked woman squirming in a casket; when his mother sensed his guilt at what he had seen, he "forgot the guilt of the tent for the nameless unplaced guilt that was in him." In the first chapter Haze's coffin dream in the pullman berth climaxes with the recollection of his mother's face as the coffin lid is closed on her. Other related images are his mother's "shiffer-robe" and the privy/toilet stall: he finds Mrs. Watts's name in a toilet stall, and his first idea of what he would see in the sideshow was "something about a privy . . . maybe it's a man and a woman in a privy."

The woman's reflection in the mummy case evokes both the sideshow experience and Haze's other "nameless" guilt—possibly the sin committed before he had committed blasphemy or fornication. "There's no person a whoremonger, who wasn't something worse first," Haze said. "That's not the sin, nor blasphemy. The sin came before them" (p. 45).

Sabbath's maternal response to the "new jesus" naturally awakens in Haze's mind associations with sin and with death. In the bedroom scene when she presents her "child" to him, mirrors and reflections are as important as in the museum scene with Enoch. When Enoch first arrives with the mummy, Haze is asleep and Sabbath is "studying herself in a pocket mirror." While she is out of the room, Haze begins packing his duffel bag and finds his mother's glasses, which he had forgotten he owned; meantime, Sabbath unwraps the mummy and, in response to the "trace of a grin covering his terrified look," she rocks the mummy and "a slight reflection of the same grin appeared on her own face." " 'Who's your momma and daddy?' she asked," and "an answer came to her mind at once."

Sabbath takes the mummy to Haze's room to "give him a jolt." Wearing his mother's glasses, Haze is looking into the wall mirror, when "the door opened and two more faces floated into his line of vision." The faces are Sabbath's and the mummy's; eventually, Haze tears the mummy from the girl's arms and throws it against the wall before throwing it out the door and into the rain. Sabbath accuses Haze of being mean and evil—"mean anough to slam a baby against a wall"—and she rightly interprets what Haze has done: "I seen you wouldn't never have no fun or let anybody else because you didn't want nothing but Jesus." In response Haze shouts, "I've seen the only truth there is" (p. 103).

The chapter concludes with his removing his mother's glasses and throwing them out the door. Just before Sabbath's entry with the "new jesus," Haze, wearing the "little silver-rimmed glasses," saw "his mother's face in his, looking at the face in the mirror." The glasses make Sabbath and the mummy, though they are only about four feet away, seem "just under his eyes." Destroying the mummy, which he sees through the distorting spectacles, is an important step toward Haze's achievement of true vision.

Wise Blood is also a novel of passage. Its movement is from confinement to freedom, from darkness of night at the beginning to light of day at the end. Haze's claustrophobic state in his berth foreshadows a series of cage images, all related to the confinement of spirit in flesh. The entire opening sequence aboard a train foreshadows the tunnel image used at the end of the book. Protagonist and reader enter a dark passageway with a pinpoint of light visible at the opposite end: although Haze disappears in the "dark tunnel," he becomes Mrs. Flood's pinpoint of light. Thus the symbolic passageway unfolds man's movement from perversion to grace.

Haze's perversion is twofold, for he is neither physically nor spiritually whole. He seeks women not for pleasure but for sin, in contrast to his childhood resolution to avoid sin for the purpose of avoiding Jesus. In chapter one Miss O'Connor evokes one of Haze's grandfather's sermons containing the prediction that "Jesus would have him in the end." She adds, "The boy didn't need to hear it. There was already a black wordless conviction in him that the way to avoid Jesus was to avoid sin. He knew by the time he was twelve years old that he was going to be a preacher" (p. 16). However, when Haze sees Mrs. Leora Watts's name and address on the wall of a toilet stall, he goes directly to her house. Ironically, by seeking what he regards as sinful, Haze is seeking Jesus.

On the train, dozing in his upper berth, Haze dreams of his mother's returning from the dead, unsatisfied. Waking from his dream, he cries out: " 'I'm sick! I can't be closed up in this thing. Get me out!' The porter stood watching him and didn't move. 'Jesus,' Haze said, 'Jesus.' The porter didn't move. 'Jesus been a long time gone,' he said in a sour triumphant voice" (p. 19). Haze's call to (or for) Jesus may be blasphemous, but the porter takes his call as a literal plea for divine help. The porter, who had earlier snubbed Haze's attempts to make conversation, offers no help. Haze's identification of him as a "Parrum nigger from Eastrod," establishes him as the first of a series of men Haze meets who are "not true," that is, not what they seem to be. His sour triumph that "Jesus been a long time gone" suggests his materialistic value scale which has resulted from his "rising" above his origins and denying his background.

The reversal, the triumph of spiritual over physical values, occurs in the last chapter. Haze, who had earlier believed implicitly in his automobile and its power to take him to another city and away from his crime of murder, "gets out" on foot, saying, "There's no other house nor no other city." Mrs. Flood, who wishes to take care of him in his blindness, responds: "There's nothing Mr. Motes . . . and time goes forward, it don't go backward and unless you take what's offered you, you'll find yourself out in the cold pitch black and just how far do you think you'll get?" (p. 124). Though in fact Haze does not get far, he chooses the "cold pitch black" rather than the physical comfort and security offered him by Mrs. Flood, whose interest in him has progressed from material avarice through physical desire to spiritual self-seeking. Even before he is brought home dead, she has been affected by his sacrifice. Thinking of her life and "coming to the last part of it," she longs for Haze's return; though she is incapable of understanding his self-mortification, particularly his blinding himself, she partially understands the value of his blindness to her: "If she was going to be blind when she was dead, who better to guide her than a blind man? Who better to lead the blind than the blind, who knew what it was like?" (p. 125).

Two days after his departure from Mrs. Flood's house, Haze is found half dead by two policemen who can barely determine that his suit, once glaring in color, is blue. Blue is traditionally associated with truth; appropriately, when the policemen find Haze, the rain has ceased and the clouds are dispelled. His faded blue suit and the appearance of blue in the sky both suggest that the "haze" has also been dispelled through his choice of spiritual over physical values. Haze Motes's physical vision had prevented his attaining spiritual vision; repeating the basic Christian paradox, Miss O'Connor underscores the necessity of losing one's life to find it.

The policemen tell Haze that he must return to Mrs. Flood's house to pay his rent. She has lied, but her lie also serves the purposes of truth. Haze Motes's "rent" is his payment for material shelter, or the price of physical existence: his experience "redeems," or pays for, his life when he becomes his landlady's pinpoint of light.

In chapter two, on his way to Mrs. Watts's house, Haze argues with a cab driver who calls him a preacher. Haze snaps back: " 'I'm not a preacher. . . . Listen, get this: I don't believe in anything.' " "The driver closed his mouth and after a second he returned the piece of cigar to it. 'That's the trouble with you preachers,' he said. 'You've all got too good to believe in anything,' and he drove off with a look of disgust and righteousness" (pp. 21, 22). The cab driver recognizes, as does Asa Hawks, that Haze is "Jesus hungry," and Haze's denials of his belief, both in words and in action, mark him as another character who is "not true." The porter who denies his origins and his religion is no worse in his negation than Haze.

On the opposite side of the novel's structural arch, in chapter thirteen, Haze speeds out of town chasing his "double," Solace Layfield, a combination of the characters Enoch and Haze, who has been preaching from a "rat-colored car" like Haze's. Haze forces Solace to strip off his blue suit (exactly like Haze's), for he knows that Solace is "not true." He drives his Essex automobile over Solace, thereby symbolically destroying Solace's perverted nature. He tells his victim: "You ain't true. . . . You believe in Jesus. Two things I can't stand —a man that ain't true and one that mocks what is" (p. 111).

The destruction of his car follows Haze's murder of Solace. The choice of the Essex is suggestive: *is sex*. A policeman pushes the car over a cliff in a scene that recalls Christ's driving the devil-infested swine into the sea. (Miss O'Connor's details in this scene, combined with her earlier use of the scriptural passage in the story "The River," support such a reading.) The policeman tells Haze he will "see better" if he gets out of the car, and indeed he does see better. After the car plunges over the bank, Haze insists that he is going nowhere and refuses the policeman's offer of a ride; then he returns to the city and buys the lime with which to blind himself. He is sickened by the sight of the visible world, and with the destruction of the car he has finally realized he is going nowhere.

Chapters three, four, and five of *Wise Blood* introduce three important minor characters—Enoch Emery, Asa Hawks, and Sabbath Lily—all of whom have perverted natures. Asa Hawks—whose feigned self-sacrifice as a Christlike man makes him *as a* hawk—sells religion in front of a department store where he takes advantage of a potato-peeler salesman's crowd. His last name combines a suggestion of Christ (as in Gerard Manley Hopkins's "The Windhover") and the literal meaning "to sell by calling out in the street." He wears dark glasses to cover his eyes, which he claims to have put out as testimony to his belief in Jesus. Ironically, Hawks tells Haze, "You got eyes and see not, ears and hear not, but you'll have to see sometime" (p. 33). Later Haze will recognize the importance of what Hawks tells him, but his first response is that he does not need Jesus since he has Leora Watts, whose name implies the power of the purely carnal.

Sabbath Lily is Hawks's bastard daughter; she is well schooled in evil, and her nature totally belies her name. She acts as the "blind" Hawks's guide until she meets Haze, for whom she waits in bed hoping to snare a husband. Sabbath pathetically mothers the "new jesus" when Enoch Emery brings it to Haze. Haze rejects it with the same gesture with which he hurls his mother's glasses away, but Sabbath neither knows nor cares that the "new jesus" is bloodless and dry.

Enoch's name suggests a reversal of evolution, a suggestion that recurs with his ritual procession past the caged animals at the zoo. In the Old Testament Enoch was the father of Methuselah; emery is an abrasive. From the corruptible Enoch in the Old Testament came the incorruptible son; similarly, from the human Enoch in *Wise Blood* comes the gorilla "Gonga." Enoch first appears in chapter three, part one; on the opposite side of the structural arch, in chapter twelve, part three, he assumes the form of his inner nature when he dons the stolen gorilla suit.

Of the three minor characters, Enoch is by far the most important, for he serves as Haze's counterpart throughout the novel. Alone in the world, he escapes the welfare woman who is trying to "save" him and flees to Taulkinham. He meets Haze at the potato-peeler salesman's stand and tries in vain to become Haze's friend; Haze is more interested in following Asa Hawks, who is wandering down the street. Enoch's concern with the physical is indicated by his desire to go with Haze to a whorehouse and, more subtly, by his preventing Haze's walking into a passing car. Enoch's eyesight is bad, but he sees the physical danger to which Haze is oblivious.

Enoch tells Haze of his escape from the welfare woman, who sent him to a Bible academy where he thought he was going "to be sancti-fied crazy": he had displayed himself naked to her, nearly frighten-ing her to death. Whether stripped or encumbered with the gorilla suit, Enoch embodies the needs of the flesh; he is still confined physically in an alien world though he has escaped the hated Bible academy. He seeks friendship and is rejected; desperate for human contact, he begs Haze to accompany him to a whorehouse. As Haze leaves him, Enoch says, "People ain't friendly here. You ain't from here but you ain't friendly neither. . . . You don't know nobody nei-ther . . . you ain't got no woman nor nothing to do. I knew when I first seen you you didn't have nobody nor nothing but Jesus. I seen you and I knew it" (p. 36). Enoch knows that Haze is not true, but despite his knowledge, he represents man's regression. Miss O'Connor's parallel development of the two men in chapter three underlines her use of the character Enoch. Enoch has already yielded to what Haze struggles against—total confinement in the physical—and Enoch's eventual fate emphasizes his total immersion in animalism. He personifies what Haze might become if he does not learn the truth.

On the opposite side of the structural arch, chapter twelve, Enoch remains both comic and pathetic as he buries his clothes and dons the gorilla suit. Earlier he had stood in a line with children in front of a theater to shake the hand of the "star Gonga" so that he could in-sult "a successful ape," but then he realized that "it was the first hand that had been extended to him since he had come to the city." Clasping the hairy hand, he tried to introduce himself, repeating exactly what he had said to Haze. But "Gonga" leaned forward and a change came into his eyes: "an ugly pair of human ones moved closer and squinted at Enoch from behind the celluloid pair. 'You go to hell,' a surly voice inside the apesuit said, low but distinctly, and the hand jerked away." Enoch's humiliation sent him running "off into the rain as fast as he could" (pp. 98, 99).

Besides its relevance to the novel's theme, the Gonga passage is important in understanding the climax of Enoch's actions in chapter twelve. The passage recalls earlier quests resulting in insult and rejection. The emphasis on vision is restated, as in the passageway, which here becomes "You go to hell." Enoch's rushing out into the rain also foreshadows his "end," parallel to that of Haze. Recall that in the final chapter Mrs. Flood in effect tells Haze—rushing out into the rain—to go to hell: "Unless you take what's offered you, you'll find yourself out in the cold pitch black."

Enoch's symbolic embodiment as the "new jesus" is foreshadowed in the opening lines of chapter twelve: "In spite of himself, Enoch couldn't get over the expectation that the new jesus was going to do something for him in return for his services. This was the virtue of Hope, which was made up, in Enoch, of two parts suspicion and one part lust" (p. 104). Enoch's suspicion is to be fulfilled; setting out on his mission, he feels that he is "after some honor" which he may have to "snatch," as he had to steal the "new jesus" from the museum. Carrying a weapon, he stops at a restaurant where he borrows part of a newspaper from a man who offers him the comic section—his favorite. On the reverse side of the comics Enoch discovers an announcement of the "last appearance in the city" of "Gonga, Giant Jungle Monarch" at the Victory Theater. "If anyone had watched Enoch read this, he would have seen a certain transformation in his countenance. It still shone with the inspiration he had absorbed from the comic strips, but something else had come over it: a look of awakening" (p. 105).

Hurrying toward the literal and symbolic Victory, Enoch, with his "squint fixed on the glary spot," remains on the opposite side of the street waiting to get into the back door of Gonga's truck, where he wrestles with the "animal" while the unaware driver climbs into the cab and drives off. Enoch's regression is clearly a reversal of Haze's early struggle in the confinement of the pullman berth. (However, Haze's struggle extends as, attempting to deny his belief, he argues with the cab driver who delivers him to Leora Watts.)

Jumping from the van with the gorilla suit, Enoch "limped hurriedly off toward the woods." Burning with the "intensest kind of happiness," he took off his clothes and buried them. To make it impossible for the reader to misinterpret the action, Miss O'Connor adds: "Burying his clothes was not a symbol of burying his former self; he only knew he wouldn't need them any more." She leaves no room for belief that the monkey suit is a temporary disguise: Enoch has assumed the outer garb appropriate to his inner nature. (She provides no such explanation, however, when Haze forces Solace to strip off his clothes and runs over him with the Essex.) Equally clear are the preparations for Enoch's "return": "It began to growl and beat its chest; it jumped up and down and flung its arms and thrust its head forward. The growls were thin and uncertain at first but they grew louder after a second. They became low and poisonous, louder again, low and poisonous again; they stopped altogether. The figure extended its hand, clutched nothing, and shook its arm vigorously; it withdrew the arm, extended it again, clutched nothing, and shook. It repeated this four or five times." Enoch's dress rehearsal implies an eventual debut. Instinctively realizing that man extends his hand only toward the animal (symbolically, the material), Enoch rehearses for his role as "friend" to the material-oriented world and prepares for reentry in bestial form. "No gorilla in existence, whether in the jungles of Africa or California or in New York City in the finest apartment in the world, was happier at that moment than this one, whose god had finally rewarded it" (pp. 107, 108).

This is the end of Enoch's story, his horrifying yet hilarious rebirth as the "new jesus" in animal form. He walks with outstretched hand toward a couple "sitting close together on a rock just off the highway"; apparently lovers, they do not see the "gorilla" approaching. "The young man turned his neck just in time to see the gorilla standing a few feet away, hideous and black, with its hand extended. He eased his arm from around the woman and disappeared silently into the woods"; the girl then runs screaming down the highway. Ironically, the lovers flee from the sight of an animal form, unaware of their own inward animalistic nature; their vision is limited to external form. They leave Enoch "surprised," a rather pathetic character dropping his arms to his side—much like a real gorilla—and sitting down on the rock to stare "over the valley at the uneven skyline of the city" (p. 108). It is because Miss O'Connor believed that man's vision is limited to the external and the material that she gives her readers a symbolic "new jesus" in bestial form.

She has been criticized for leaving Enoch's story "unfinished," but it is in fact finished, and the critics have missed the whole significance of the character by failing to realize why he has been left looking out over the city. Enoch himself is the "new jesus" created by modern man in a materialistic world where his perverse inclinations deny spiritual fulfillment. Haze comes to see this danger and blinds himself, thus gaining spiritual insight. Enoch, living in isolation and motivated by animal instincts alone, accepts the beastly role. He is man in his lowest, most perverted state. Miss O'Connor apparently borrowed Yeats's "rough beast slouching toward Bethlehem" ("The Second Coming"), for she purposely leaves Enoch sitting on the outskirts of town in order to suggest his eventual return.[5] Enoch's response to his "daddy's wise blood," his purely physiological nature, culminates in his alienation and dehumanization.

A return to part one—where Haze's perverse inclinations are indicated by the purchase of the Essex and his dalliance with Leora Watts—finds him visiting the city park to get Hawks's address from Enoch. Chapter five opens: "That morning Enoch Emery knew when he woke up that today the person he could show it to was going to come. He knew by his blood. He had wise blood like his daddy" (p. 46). Enoch takes Haze's arrival in the Essex as the "sign" for him to share his discovery of a shriveled mummy in a coffin-like case in the park museum. Daily visits to the mummy climax Enoch's ritualistic glorification of the physical and the "dirty"; he also hides in the park to watch the women swim and makes suggestive remarks to the waitress.

On the way to the museum Haze and Enoch must stop for a soda, for the taking of refreshment is part of Enoch's ritual. The waitress tells Haze that "there ain't anything sweeter than a clean boy. God for my witness . . . I know a clean boy when I see one." Haze shouts, "I AM clean . . . if Jesus existed, I wouldn't be clean" (p. 53). Haze's denial is partly a response to his childhood guilt when his mother made him feel dirty for what he had done; because he also associates Jesus with dirt and sin he asserts, "I AM clean."

On the opposite side of the arch, in part three, Haze sees himself in Solace Layfield, an untrue prophet. Solace, who needs money to support his wife and children, is hired by Hoover Shoats to act as an evangelist. Shoats—the name means hogs and suggests sensuality and gluttony—is interested only in making money and taking revenge on Haze through preaching the Church Without Christ. He calls Solace the "true prophet" and has him dress like Haze.

With seeming irrelevance Haze replies to a spectator who asks if he and Solace are twins, "If you don't hunt it down and kill it, it'll hunt you down and kill you" (p. 91). He alludes to his conscience, but the answer also recalls a note he had left in the only material possession remaining in his home when he returned from the Army (part one): "THIS SHIFFER-ROBE BELONGS TO HAZE MOTES. DO NOT STEAL IT OR YOU WILL BE HUNTED DOWN AND KILLED" (p. 19). Because Solace is not true he pricks Haze's conscience; the "shiffer-robe" links his conscience with his mother again, for she had paid thirty dollars for the piece of furniture (which, appropriately, reiterates the box pattern). Although Haze thinks that killing Solace will destroy his conscience, the act will instead set him free for redemption—making him a Christian *malgré lui*.

After he murders Solace Layfield, Haze lines the bottoms of his shoes with rocks and realizes, "I'm NOT clean" (p. 122): by this time he is blind but sees the truth. He has destroyed the dried-up mummy Enoch brought him to serve as the "new jesus" for his Church Without Christ and has cast away his mother's spectacles. Recalling the meaning of the spectacles' silver rims, the evangelist's oratory, one realizes the appropriateness of Haze's ceasing to preach.

Thus, by comparing the actions balanced on either side of the structural arch, one recognizes the reversal, thematic and symbolic, in part three of the initial action in part one. The transition occurs in part two where the perversion of the Godlike and animal natures of both Enoch and Haze are further juxtaposed, then split. A brief comparison of chapters six and nine will illustrate the structural narrowing to the symbolic significance of the central chapters, seven and eight, which will also be considered together.

In chapter six Haze takes his station in front of the "picture show" to begin preaching the Church Without Christ: "I'm going to preach there was no Fall because there was nothing to fall from, and no Redemption because there was no Fall and no Judgment because there wasn't the first two. Nothing matters but that Jesus was a liar" (p. 60). Before returning to Mrs. Watts, he "preaches in front of three other picture shows."

The next morning he goes to Asa and Sabbath Lily Hawks's rooming house, rents a room, and calls on them to announce the beginning of his church. He decides to seduce Sabbath to prove he is "in earnest when he said he preached The Church Without Christ"; ironically, he does not realize that both father and daughter are far wiser in the ways of evil than he. Asa shows Haze a newspaper clipping—"Evangelist Promises to BLIND SELF"—and explains that the scars on his face were caused by the lime he used to blind himself. He does not show Haze another clipping which reads: "Evangelist's Nerve Fails" (p. 65).

In chapter nine—opposite chapter six in the arch structure— Haze sees behind the dark glasses which conceal Hawks's eyes; realizing Hawks is a fraud, he abandons the notion of seducing Sabbath. Miss O'Connor must certainly have had in mind the passage in 1 Corinthians 13 on seeing through a glass darkly, for Hawks's glasses prevent Haze's seeing the truth and Hawks himself sees "darkly" in at least a double metaphoric sense. Again Haze has gone to preach the Church Without Christ, this time in front of four picture shows. That night his "disciple," Hoover Shoats, whose assumed name is Onnie Jay Holy, has appeared. The two names together suggest the disciple's hypocrisy: he assumes an attitude of holiness to conceal an animal nature, and when he preaches to Haze's audience, he emphasizes the doctrine of innate goodness and the power of religion to enable one to win friends. Like Enoch, Shoats is animalistic but values human friendship above all else. The value he places on friendship and religion is purely mercenary. Pretending to be Haze's assistant, Shoats, like Hawks, attempts to sell religion: "It'll cost you each a dollar but what is a dollar? A few dimes! Not too much to pay to unlock that little rose of sweetness inside you!" (p. 85). Haze shouts, "You ain't true," and returns to the rooming house, where he picks the lock of Hawks's room in order to see into the false prophet's eyes; thus he discovers that Hawks is not really blind: "Haze squatted down by him and struck a match close to his face and he opened his eyes. The two sets of eyes looked at each other as long as the match lasted; Haze's expression seemed to open onto a deeper blankness and reflect something and then close again" (p. 89).

In chapter seven, devoted primarily to Haze, his first doubt of his mission occurs when he and Sabbath drive to the country. On the way she tells him that she is a bastard. He cannot understand "how a preacher who had blinded himself for Jesus could have a bastard." As Sabbath continues to talk, Haze tries four times to interrupt for an explanation. "How could you be. . . ," "Listen here, if he blinded himself, how. . . ," "Your daddy blinded himself," he says, revealing his envy of Hawks's faith. He asks Sabbath, "Was he a very evil-seeming man before he came to believe . . . or just part way evil-seeming?" She replies: "All the way evil" (pp. 66–68). Haze's response, "I suppose before he came to believe he didn't believe at all," reveals his capacity for insight.

His realization determines him to return to town, but car trouble requires that he walk to a gas pump where he sees a cage with a sign over it: "TWO DEADLY ENEMIES. HAVE A LOOK FREE." Haze walks over to the cage: "There was a black bear about four feet long and very thin, resting on the floor of the cage; his back was spotted with bird lime that had been shot down on him by a small chicken hawk that was sitting on a perch in the upper part of the same apartment. Most of the hawk's tail was gone; the bear had only one eye" (p. 70). The caged animals prefigure Haze's end. A black bear (symbolizing evil influence), though capable of walking erect, lies on the floor accepting the pelleting of the hawk (representative of Christ), who sits perched on high. The bear's one eye suggests the effect of grace, for as Saint Matthew writes: "The light of the body is the eye: if therefore, thine eye be single, thy whole body shall be full of light" (Matt. 6:22). But the hawk, missing part of his tail, has undergone violence in "conquering" the bear. This scene recalls an earlier scene at the zoo, in chapter five, when Enoch took Haze past the animal cages—first the bears, then the wolves (which Enoch thought were hyenas); finally, "rushing" by the monkeys and "running" past the birds, Enoch looked back to discover Haze gazing into the one open eye of an owl as he exclaimed for the second time, "I AM clean" (p. 55). The transcendent meaning of the sign, "TWO DEADLY ENEMIES. HAVE A LOOK FREE," epitomizes the theme of the book: man's animal nature requires mortification and submission to grace.

In chapter eight the split between Haze and his counterpart Enoch is foreshadowed, alerting the reader to the eventual triumph of animal nature in Enoch. Again the action is predominantly symbolic. The chapter opens with Enoch's knowledge that "his life would never be the same again, because the thing that was going to happen . . . had started to happen when he showed what was in the glass case to Haze Motes." For Enoch the knowledge is a "mystery beyond understanding," but he knows that what will happen will be awful. "His blood was more sensitive than any other part of him; it wrote doom all through him" (p. 72). Enoch's wise blood foretells his symbolic "collapse" in chapter twelve when he waits on the outskirts of town.

He begins a sacrificial cleansing ritual which involves saving his money (eating less), cleaning his room, and scrubbing his furniture. He prepares a "washstand," "a tabernacle-like cabinet which was meant to contain a slop-jar," by painting it gilt. Ironically, for he does not know why, he prepares a space for the tangible but dry "jesus." "On the following Monday, he was certain when he woke up that today was the day he was going to know on. His blood was rushing around. . . . When he realized that today was the day, he decided not to get up. He didn't want to justify his daddy's blood, he didn't want to be always having to do something that something else wanted him to do. . . . Naturally his blood was not going to put up with any attitude like this. He was at the zoo by nine-thirty" (p. 75). Enoch's animal nature has reached that state of perversion which permits it to govern his conscious desires. His Godlike nature is completely submerged, and he seems driven to do things he had rather not: "I ain't going to do it, he said and stopped. He had stopped in front of a movie house" (p. 77).

The movie house recurs frequently in the book: its dark cavern, with the only light cast on a screen, encloses masses of people. The artificial reality—the delusion—of the movies, combined with the fact that films serve as vicarious experience for most modern men, makes it particularly appropriate that Miss O'Connor uses movie theaters in this way. The art of montage creates the illusion of reality, which serves the modern age far better than does truth, for cinematic reality speaks chiefly to the physical eye. Haze is preaching outside the picture show, and Enoch, although trying to resist, finds himself entombed inside, where his "revelation" comes during a triple feature.

Just as the symbols of the "deadly enemies" in chapter seven foreshadow Haze's ultimate end, the remainder of Enoch's story is foretold symbolically through the three movies he sees. The first movie, about "the Eye who performed operations by remote control," is an obvious allusion to the symbols of the one-eyed bear (light) in the previous chapter and the one-eyed owl in chapter five. But Enoch's vision is to be in a different direction from Haze's. The second movie, "about life at Devil's Island Penitentiary," alludes again to the caged "deadly enemies" and to the caged animals at the zoo. It also represents Enoch's future "home." The third movie, called "Lonnie Comes Home Again," is about a baboon named Lonnie. This last title establishes the split in the Godlike and animal natures shared by Haze and Enoch, for Enoch later assumes animal form by donning the gorilla suit, and on the last page, as predicted on the first, Haze "goes home." The three movies symbolize Enoch's regression from light, to confinement, to the beastly form—the "baboon Lonnie" who will be left on the outskirts of town to "come home again." In contrast, the "deadly enemies" in chapter seven symbolize Haze's story: the black "animal," defeated by the "hawk," sees the light. The animal nature and the Godlike nature are compatible only when the two are integrated and neither dominates the other.

When Enoch leaves the theater he hears Haze preaching: "The Church Without Christ don't have a Jesus but it needs one! It needs a new jesus! It needs one that's all man, without blood to waste, and it needs one that don't look like any other man so you'll look at him. Give me such a jesus, you people. Give me such a new jesus and you'll see how far the Church Without Christ can go!" (p. 78). Enoch suddenly realizes that he can provide the "new jesus." He whispers, "Listen here, I got him! I mean I can get him! You know! Him! Him I shown you to. You seen him yourself" (p. 79). The mummy's importance to Enoch is such that he fails to realize it is an insentient object.

In part three Haze destroys the mummy, but Enoch puts on the lifeless, bloodless gorilla suit; thus Enoch himself becomes the symbol of the "new jesus," who has no blood to waste and does not "look like any other man." We must look at him, however, and we realize that he is much like Yeats's "rough beast slouching toward Bethlehem" that suggests the end of the Christian era. But on the last page Miss O'Connor provides an alternative through Haze, who becomes a "pin point of light."

In some of her critical notes about her own writing, Miss O'Connor made explicit the importance of Haze's final belief in Christ. For instance, in her note introducing the Signet edition of the novel, 3 *by Flannery O'Connor,* she spoke of readers for whom belief in Christ is "a matter of no great consequence. For them, Haze Motes' integrity lies in his trying with such vigor to get rid of the ragged figure who moves from tree to tree in the back of his mind. For the author, his integrity lies in his not being able to. Does one's integrity ever lie in what he is not able to do? I think that usually it does, for free will does not mean one will, but many wills conflicting in one man." Miss O'Connor regards freedom as a mystery which "cannot be conceived simply"; "a novel, even a comic novel, can be asked only to deepen" that mystery. In another context, excerpts from letters written to Winifred McCarthy (*Mystery and Manners,* pp. 115–18), Miss O'Connor again alludes to her view of free will.

In those letters, collected under the title "In the Devil's Territory," she appears to allude to Haze Motes, though she does not name him, when she writes, "The Catholic novelist believes that you destroy your freedom by sin; the modern reader believes, I think, that you gain it that way." She then writes that old Tarwater (the hero of *The Violent Bear It Away*) "is certainly free and meant to be; if he appears to have a compulsion to be a prophet, I can only insist that in this compulsion there is the mystery of God's will for him, and that it is not compulsion in the clinical sense." "As for Enoch," she continues, "he is a moron and chiefly a comic character. I don't think it is important whether his compulsion is clinical or not."

With those words Miss O'Connor clarifies her intentions and rights the balance between Enoch Emery's story and Haze Motes's story. Enoch Emery's wise blood prompts him to return to the animal state, but Haze, for all his efforts, is unable to escape the "ragged figure who moves from tree to tree in the back of his mind." Haze's integrity lies in his very inability to escape, and the message comes forth with singular force: not a return to the animal but an overcoming of the animal will permit man at last to come home.

CHAPTER FOUR

The Expanded Vision

From the Tower of Babel to Vicarious Atonement

IN A GOOD MAN IS HARD TO FIND, as in her final collection of stories, Miss O'Connor employs a framing device similar to the novelistic structure she perfected in her two longer works of fiction, *Wise Blood* and *The Violent Bear It Away*. The fact that both collections conclude with stories totally revised from their earlier published forms supports the idea of her conscious use of a frame as a fictional device.

Miss O'Connor's cumulative meaning in *A Good Man Is Hard to Find* goes far beyond an indictment of man for his innate depravity: her stories about original sin are stories of hope, for when her characters admit the existence of evil in themselves and in others, they are left to look into their hearts and souls, perhaps even to seek redemption. One is again reminded of the debt to Mauriac.

As the epigraph suggests, the stories in the collection are about travelers, and, while the individual stories dramatize their passing the dragon, the collection as a whole accomplishes a doctrinal progression: it goes from the Tower of Babel, realized symbolically in the title story, to the vicarious atonement, realized in the concluding story, "The Displaced Person." More than a collection of stories about grotesques, as it has been called, *A Good Man Is Hard to Find* achieves thematic unity of the sort usually accomplished only in the novel. The separate stories deal with characters whose traits make them part of Miss O'Connor's fictional family; their individual experiences unite them with mankind despite their superficial differences.

To deal first with the unifying device of motion, specifically automation, one observes that the characters in the title story are on vacation, bound for Florida, and the Misfit, whom they encounter because of an automobile accident, is fleeing from justice after escaping from a federal penitentiary. In the second story, "The River," little Harry Ashfield drowns himself in what he considers "the river of life," which he hopes will take him to "the Kingdom of Christ" so he will not have to go back to his drunken parents' apartment. The travel motif is repeated in the title of another story, "The Life You Save May Be Your Own," in which the one-armed itinerant handyman Mr. Shiftlet says, "The body, lady, is like a house; it don't go anywhere: but the spirit, lady, is like a automobile: always on the move, always" (p. 166). At the end of the story Mr. Shiftlet has his automobile and abandons the "Angel of Gawd" (poor, simpleminded Lucynell Crater), to race a turnip-shaped cloud toward Mobile.[1]

The travel pattern continues: in "A Temple of the Holy Ghost" two silly girls studying at a convent visit a relative; the story's most important character, symbolically, is a freak in a traveling show, and the last image is a "red clay road hanging over the trees." Significantly, the road has been left in the sky by the passage of a giant red sun which looks like "an elevated Host drenched in blood." "The Artificial Nigger" also centers on a journey, Nelson's first visit to Atlanta with his grandfather, old Mr. Head. In "A Circle in the Fire," on the other hand, city boys come to the country, where they burn Mrs. Cope's precious trees.

In "A Late Encounter with the Enemy" an old Confederate soldier, immobilized in his wheelchair at his granddaughter's graduation, is overwhelmed by a succession of places—Chickamauga, Shiloh, Marthasville—which "rushed at him as if the past were the only future now and he had to endure it." The moment of his death is realized in terms of time and place and eternity, which somehow meet; just before he dies, 'General' Sash strains to "find out what comes after the past." He has arrived at his eternal crossroads, just as do many of Miss O'Connor's characters.

In "Good Country People" a door-to-door Bible salesman, who admits that he doesn't stay in any place long, shatters Joy (Hulga) Hopewell's pride in her religious negation. "The Displaced Person," linked internally with "A Good Man Is Hard to Find," introduces a European, a victim of the atrocities of the Second World War, into a Georgia farm setting. His effect on Mrs. Shortley, the wife of a shiftless tenant farmer, is drastic: in her fury at him she dies of a stroke, but her eyes opened in death and "seemed to contemplate for the first time the tremendous frontiers of her true country" (p. 280). Two other characters in the story, though they do not die, are altered to the extent that they are "taken with a sudden desire to see more of the world" and leave the farm.

One story in the collection appears at first sight not to fit into the travel theme; it is "A Stroke of Good Fortune," a story usually dismissed by the critics. Stanley Edgar Hyman regards the story as a "leaden tract against complacency and contraception" (*Flannery O'Connor*, p. 19), and Jane Hart, an early and generally perceptive reader, wrote that "on the whole, 'A Stroke of Good Fortune' does not come to much."[2] In fact the story may come to a great deal, though it does so by moving not horizontally but vertically—rising on steps that "stuck straight up like steeple steps" (p. 172).

In "A Stroke of Good Fortune" Ruby Hill, mounting her apartment house steps and longing for the convenience of the suburbs, loses her complacency when she comes to realize that her husband has failed to "take care of that," and she is pregnant. Awareness of the life in her leads to awareness also of something outside her. She does not get to her apartment at the top of the stairs, for she is intercepted by History (goatlike Mr. Jerger) and visits Carnality (vulgar Laverne Watts). Jerger, a history teacher, questions her about an important birthday, the discovery of Florida in 1516, but Ruby is not interested until he mentions the fabled Fountain of Youth; she is extremely conscious of her age and of the advantages of remaining young. She loses interest again when she learns that Ponce de Leon did not find the fountain and that Mr. Jerger, who claims to have drunk the miraculous water, had searched for it in his heart. Above Jerger's floor the steps become "darker and steeper"; nauseated, Ruby staggers into Laverne Watts's apartment, where the unmarried but worldly-wise woman teases her about being pregnant. Laverne shows off her new shoes and suggests, lasciviously, that she would like to show them to Ruby's brother Rufus who is home on furlough from the European Theater. Ruby is shocked, for she regards her brother as a baby; she has thought of him as unborn but "waiting out nowhere before he was born, just waiting, waiting to make his mother, only thirty-four, into an old woman." Ruby is thirty-four. Elsewhere she imagines Rufus waiting "nowhere" to make his mother "a little deader" (p. 181).

Such is the context of Ruby's realization of her pregnancy. Earlier she had sat on little Hartley Gilfeet's toy pistol, "nine inches of treacherous tin," and recalled that Hartley's mother calls him "Little Mister Good Fortune" because the child is all her husband left her when he died. At the story's end she is able to reject her fatuous interpretation of a fortuneteller's message that her illness is a "stroke of good fortune": because she had wanted to leave the city for the suburbs, Ruby had decided that her illness would force her husband to move. Her faith in Madam Zoleeda gone, she says, "Good Fortune, Baby," and the words echo back to her from three flights of stairs: "Then she recognized the feeling again, a little roll. It was as if it were not in her stomach. It was as if it were out nowhere in nothing, out nowhere, resting and waiting, with plenty of time" (p. 182). For all her progressive and enlightened views revealed earlier in the story, Ruby is not different from her mother, and she comes to understand in her upward movement that she is subject to all the "disorders" of woman. Procreation is a result of the fall, part of the terms of human existence, as is the other inescapable fact of death. Her life as she has lived it is over; the life inside her testifies to something outside her "resting and waiting, with plenty of time."

The importance of the travel theme in the collection is apparent. The travelers reach their internal realizations of grace, but frequently they do so only after they have reached the Father of Souls by leaving the dragon of secularism behind. For example, in the second story, after Harry Ashfield has been swept away by the river, the "monster," Mr. Paradise, remains behind looking downriver with his "dull eyes" as far as he can see. Paradise judges everything in material terms. His rough call interrupts the faith-healing service: "Pass the hat and give this kid his money. That's what he's here for."

"The River" focuses on a child, Harry Ashfield, sent home with the babysitter, Mrs. Connin, while his parents recover from a hangover. Hearing Mrs. Connin speak of her preacher, Bevel Summers, Harry identifies with him, insisting that his name is Bevel also. Even before he meets the preacher, the boy assumes a new identity. Later Harry sees pigs close at hand for the first time when Mrs. Connin's sons trick him into releasing the animals. Mrs. Connin tells him one hog "favors Mr. Paradise," whom he will see at the faith-healing service; she shows Harry pictures of Jesus driving evil spirits from a man into a herd of swine. The scene at the river where Harry is baptized suggests John the Baptist's ministry, for Bevel Summers, like John, denies that he has healing or redemptive powers: "This old red suffering stream goes on, you people, slow to the Kingdom of Christ. This old red river is good to baptize in, good to lay your faith in, good to lay your pain in, but it ain't this muddy water here that saves you" (p. 152). The "slow circles of two silent birds revolving high in the air" attest to the sanctity of the scene; at length, they dropped "lightly in the top of the highest pine and sat hunch-shouldered as if they were supporting the sky." Though he does not understand the sacrament, Harry agrees to be baptized when the preacher asks if he wants to be "washed in the river of suffering"; afterward he thinks: "I won't have to go back to the apartment then, I'll go under the river."

When he does return to his parents' apartment, Harry reveals one of Miss O'Connor's recurrent signs of grace, sight through a single eye: "one of Bevel's eyes was closed and the other, half closed." (The one-eyed hawk and the owl with one eye open embody the same meaning in *Wise Blood*.) Bevel's single sight is modified by another detail; he has stolen Mrs. Connin's Bible-story book and hidden it in his coat lining: "the damp plain cloth dragged down on one side." Judging the age and value of the book, his parents' friends take it from the boy and he is unable to find it the next morning.

Stealing carfare and slipping away from home, the boy returns to the river and splashes hopefully into the water: "His coat floated to the surface and surrounded him like a strange gay lily pad and he stood grinning in the sun." The water does not take him away until, hearing a shout, he turns his head and sees "something like a giant pig bounding after him, shaking a red and white club." Borne away from Mr. Paradise, Harry/Bevel is saved both from his nutty parents (as Miss O'Connor once called them) and from the candy-cane blandishments of the old secularist who follows children into the woods.

Though it appears in a different form, Miss O'Connor's dragon occurs again at the end of a later story, "A View of the Woods," and again it is associated with machinery and secular progress. For Miss O'Connor the import is clear in the final section of *The Violent Bear It Away* when a mechanized "monster," a transport truck, roars past young Tarwater. "No matter what form the dragon may take," Miss O'Connor once wrote, "it is of [the character's] mysterious passage past him, or into his jaws, that stories of any depth will always be concerned to tell" (*Mystery and Manners*, p. 35). For the most part, Miss O'Connor's stories record the victorious "passage" past the dragon, even when that passage requires death, and her dragon, no matter what its form, epitomizes human reliance on the mechanical devices of a fast-moving society which is not going anywhere until it realizes the truth.

The hunch-shouldered birds which perch in the tallest pine at Harry Ashfield's baptism preside over another scene of salvation— the destruction of Haze Motes's Essex automobile in *Wise Blood*. In "The River," the birds, though obviously vultures, remind the reader of Jesus' baptism when "the Spirit like a dove descended upon Him" (Mark 1:7, 8). In "The Role of the Catholic Novelist" Miss O'Connor wrote, "There are ages when it is possible to woo the reader; there are others when something more drastic is necessary." Apparently the vultures underscore the fact that physical death releases men from the captivity of life. In *Wise Blood* the car's destruction is witnessed by a buzzard sitting hunch-shouldered on the roof of an abandoned house; at the crash it carries some automobile trash into a clearing, then flaps "off to a tree at the edge of the clearing." One recalls Mr. Shiftlet's observation that the body is like a house; the soul, like a car. Earlier (chapter seven) Haze had seen "two deadly enemies" caged together and a cloud which looked like the traditional concept of God the Father. With his affirmation of faith in the car, the cloud had turned into a "bird with long thin wings" and disappeared in the opposite direction. Though Haze had set out in the car to go to another city after killing Solace Layfield, he was in fact not going anywhere, for the pavement appeared to be "slipping back under him." Miss O'Connor uses almost precisely the same image to describe Julian's flight toward the cluster of lights at the end of "Everything That Rises Must Converge." Her moving, restless people seek to be at rest, but their reliance on things makes their passage past the dragon unsure until things become unimportant and material progress is subordinated to inner progress.

Though Miss O'Connor termed *A Good Man Is Hard to Find* a collection of stories about original sin, she could as well have said that it is a collection of stories about redemption or mercy. For the horrible things that happen, despite their effect on the tenderhearted reader who sees physical harm as the greatest evil of all, bring her characters to realizations of themselves as limited, human creatures whose imperfections are their only hopes of spiritual salvation. The quest for redemption begins with the opening story and concludes with "The Displaced Person." In between, the characters and the reader come a little closer to the truth the Misfit in the title story wants so desperately.

The concluding stories of both collections are earlier stories, amplified and enriched. "The Displaced Person" had appeared in the *Sewanee Review* (Fall 1954), but before its appearance in the 1955 collection it had undergone a significant revision—a revision which foreshadows the technique of *The Violent Bear It Away* (1960). The original story concludes with the death of Mrs. Shortley, and as Robert Drake and other readers recognized, it is Mrs. Shortley's story. Stanley Edgar Hyman sees Mrs. Shortley as "another displaced person" (*Flannery O'Connor*, p. 17). Miss O'Connor's original story had been refreshingly ecumenical, even for the Roman Catholic writer accustomed to writing about backwoods fundamentalists: she had been content to illustrate the basic doctrine that, although Mrs. Shortley was a secularist blinded by ignorance, prejudice, and self-interest, she was not forbidden the sight of the "immense frontiers of her true country." But as good stories have a way of doing, this one grew. In the revised story Mrs. Shortley's death is but one epiphany; Mrs. McIntyre, whose red bangs and cloudy purple eyes invited further attention, represents another.

Mrs. Shortley's death is dramatized in terms which leave no doubt that it is a "good" death. Her daughters, thinking her stroke is a joke, plead to know where they are going; like Moses leading his people out of bondage, Mrs. Shortley dies before the family reaches its destination, and we are reminded that her "true country" is death. The daughter Sara Mae cannot know that Mrs. Shortley "had had a great experience or ever been displaced in the world from all that belonged to her." Mrs. Shortley's "true country" is also displacement.

Mrs. McIntyre is similarly displaced, for her "nervous affliction" leads to her acceptance of the farm's disintegration. Her story and the full import of Mr. Guizac's identification with Christ are additions to the collected story. Additions at the beginning of the story prepare for the fuller treatment of Christian redemption; for example, the peacock, explicitly associated with Christ's transfiguration and second coming, appears in the opening paragraph. Lessening the number, but not the intensity, of the opening descriptions of the mountainous Mrs. Shortley, Miss O'Connor at once contrasts the tenant woman's bulk with the peacock's delicacy and relates the two. Together they look "like a complete procession," and, notably, the bird follows the woman about on more than one occasion. In her *Sewanee Review* story Miss O'Connor employed a far less effective device to indicate Mrs. Shortley's bulk and her spiritual quality; she spoke of her bulk as adequate for carving statues of Washington and Jefferson or splashing signs of fundamentalist doctrine—and she quoted several such signs, all in capital letters.

Thus Miss O'Connor's revisions reveal characteristics of her working habits. She admitted that she never knew whether she was writing a novel or a story until she had worked the material; this long story apparently grew in very nearly the way *Wise Blood* had grown, though as it grew, Miss O'Connor emphasized structural elements other than the linear or progressive. Fusing parts two and three, Mrs. McIntyre's story, onto Mrs. Shortley's story would not have succeeded without amplifying the peacock image, which serves finally as a unifying symbol for the whole work. (Similarly, in *Wise Blood* Haze Motes's acquisition of a name, embodying two words applicable to vision, and the determination of his fate required alterations of "The Train," including the important addition of the spectacles.)

The three sections of "The Displaced Person" in revised form function largely as do the three sections of the two novels. Part two contains the elements which enable the reader to understand the meaning of Guizac's final sacrifice, of the peacocks, and of the statue on Mr. McIntyre's grave. Significantly, part two ends with Guizac's cutting diminishing circles in the fodder; Miss O'Connor writes that "by nightfall, the Displaced Person would have worked his way around and around until there would be nothing on either side of the two hills but the stubble, and down in the center, risen like a little island, the graveyard where the Judge lay grinning under his desecrated monument" (p. 289). The Displaced Person's lack of racial discrimination has already alienated his employer, and Shortley's return to the farm will seal his fate, but that fate is made meaningful by his cutting away the barrier between Mrs. McIntyre and her husband's grave, adorned with a headless angel and associated with the peacocks. The final section, containing Mrs. McIntyre's intended repudiation of her "salvation"—her "good man"—is the inevitable reversal which makes Guizac's subsequent death meaningful.

The technique in the collections as unified wholes is but slightly different; again, it is based on the relationship of the first and last sections, or stories. In both collections the final story represents a considerable doctrinal gain. The movement is from denial toward acceptance or from awareness of sin toward awareness of salvation. In "A Good Man Is Hard to Find" the title is spoken by Red Sammy Butts at The Tower, a tawdry barbecue joint, shortly before the Bailey family encounters the Misfit, who tells the grandmother that Jesus "thown [sic] everything off balance." In "The Displaced Person" Mrs. McIntyre complains that Guizac threw everything off balance, that he was "extra," but the priest says: "He came to atone for our sins."

Thus Miss O'Connor's opening story, particularly the materialistic scene at The Tower, leads inevitably to the last story and the sacrifice of Guizac, the good man who throws everything off balance because of his inability to speak English, his efficiency and hard work, and his lack of racial prejudice. One recalls that the Tower of Babel epitomizes man's vanity in physical accomplishment; attempting to raise themselves to heaven through their own efforts, men discovered that their manmade tower created divisiveness, including language differentiation. In the scene at The Tower the grandmother and Red Sammy Butts, the lazy proprietor, agree that the sorry state of world affairs is all Europe's fault. Europe, they decide, thinks America is made of money; obviously both characters regard the "sorry state of the world" in purely material terms. In her concluding story Miss

O'Connor brings a European into Georgia, where his employer regards herself as his "benefactor," expecting gratitude for the opportunity to make money for her, and Mrs. Shortley regards him with revulsion as the embodiment of all the horrors she associates with the war.

The scene at The Tower deserves closer examination. The five members of the Bailey family stop there to have lunch with Red Sammy and his tired wife. At the children's approach a monkey chained to a chinaberry tree climbs a little higher. Inside, Red Sammy is the affable host who lets his wife do the work. The grandmother wishes to dance, but her son, who lacks her "sunny disposition," glares at her. Travel makes Bailey nervous. The grandmother worries that she and her family will meet the Misfit, about whose escape from prison she has read; Mrs. Butts, who declares that she doesn't trust any man, believes that the Misfit may "attact [*sic*] this place right here" and rob her cash drawer. Red Sammy worries that he has been foolish to extend credit to two men in a good but old car and wonders why he has done it. The grandmother responds that he did it because he is a good man. "Yes'm, I suppose so," Red Sammy says, struck with her answer. Later the Misfit denies that he is a good man: " 'Nome, I ain't a good man,' The Misfit said after a second as if he had considered her statement carefully." The grandmother's response to Red Sammy reveals that she is the spokesman for a society in which goodness is linked to material things; when she calls the Misfit a good man, she adds, "You're not a bit common!" thus suggesting that goodness is somehow related to manners or to family and breeding. Even the children are corrupted by the value system she represents, for June Starr rudely points out the rundown condition of The Tower when Mrs. Butts asks if she would not like to be "her little girl." The child's answer underlines the point of The Tower scene: "I wouldn't live in a broken-down place like this for a million bucks!"

The grandmother's duplicity leads to the encounter with the Misfit, but her duplicity alone would not have caused the family's trouble had it not been for the children's inborn avarice. First the grandmother uses the story about the Misfit to persuade the family to go to Tennessee instead of Florida; when this fails, she hides her cat in the back seat. Later, after the scene at The Tower, she recalls a house which she had visited as a girl, and, wanting to see it again, she "craftily" tells the children about a secret panel that hides the family's silver. This ploy works, and the children hound their father into following her directions to the house.

The accident occurs when a "horrible thought" comes to the grandmother; they have left the highway and gone several miles before she realizes that "the house she had remembered so vividly was not in Georgia but Tennessee." Her realization makes her upset the cat's cage, and Pity Sing leaps onto Bailey's head. The resulting accident is observed by the Misfit and his henchmen; typically, it is the grandmother who flags down the Misfit's hearselike car and blurts out her recognition of him as a killer. She exaggerates the gravity of the accident, saying the car turned over three times, but the Misfit insists on the truth: the car turned over once.

The heart of "A Good Man Is Hard to Find" is the conversation between the Misfit and the grandmother while she awaits her death. She is perhaps best revealed by Miss O'Connor's observation that she always dressed for travel so that anyone finding her dead on the road would know she was a lady. Her primary concern is for externals; she is superficially genteel. She reveals the narrowness of her ethical system when she assumes that the Misfit will yield to her flattery. She assures him that he is a good man and that she can tell he comes from "good people" and thus is not "common." She begs him to pray to Jesus and assures him that if he does pray, Jesus will help him. Unfortunately, her notion of "help" is purely physical; she appeals to the Misfit's desire to stop running and settle down, but he is interested in justice, righting the imbalance between "what all I done wrong . . . [and] what all I gone through in punishment." Settling down is the grandmother's idea of the ideal life, just as her ideal former suitor was the man who bought Coca Cola shares when they were cheap. "Think how wonderful it would be to settle down and live a comfortable life," she tells the Misfit.

As her panic rises, the grandmother utters the name of Jesus as if she might be cursing and admits that perhaps Jesus did not raise the dead. She even descends to offering the Misfit money for her life, though all the other members of her family have already been killed. However, the Misfit is not concerned with comfort or with money: "Lady, there never was a body that give the undertaker a tip." He stares far beyond the grandmother into the dark woods and squats in the dust drawing circles with a stick. He is disturbed that his punishment has not suited his crimes, and he is convinced that if he had lived when Jesus lived, he would have been a different man, for then he would have known whether Jesus truly raised the dead. Like Haze Motes casting away the mummy, the Misfit wants only the truth, and like Haze, he wears silver-rimmed spectacles and looks defenseless without them.

Unlike the grandmother, whose religion was an easily acquired part of her respectability, the Misfit recognizes the magnitude of the question whether Jesus raised the dead, for "if He did what He said, then it's nothing for you to do but thow [*sic*] away everything and follow Him, and if He didn't," there's "no pleasure but meanness" (p. 142).

Just as the Misfit reaches the peak of his intense examination, the grandmother—for all her shallowness of soul—proves capable of a revelation, for she reaches out to touch him, saying, "Why, you're one of my own babies" (p. 143). The Misfit "sprang back as if a snake had bitten him and shot her three times through the chest." In one of her lectures Miss O'Connor reports trying to decide "what makes a story work, and what makes it hold up as a story." She decided that "it is probably some action, some gesture of a character that is unlike any other in the story, one which indicates where the real heart of the story lies." Such an action "would have to be on the anagogical level, that is, the level which has to do with the Divine life and our participation in it." Precisely such an action, by Miss O'Connor's own account, occurs at this point in "A Good Man Is Hard to Find": "The grandmother is at last alone, facing the Misfit. Her head clears for an instant and she realizes, even in her limited way, that she is responsible for the man before her and joined to him by ties of kinship which have their roots deep in the mystery she has been merely prattling about so far" (*Mystery and Manners*, pp. 111–12).

That gesture, she speculates, may be adequate to produce in the Misfit the pain to "turn him into the prophet he was meant to become"; but, she adds, "that's another story." As usual, Miss O'Connor's action is a prologue to the descent of grace. The grandmother's revelation, though limited, is adequate; it links her to the com-

munion of saints, which, Miss O'Connor states elsewhere, "is created upon human imperfection, created from what we make of our
grotesque state."[3] The Misfit's reaction is another gesture of the sort
Miss O'Connor describes: he springs back from the grandmother's
compassionate gesture, for that is not the truth he seeks.

Thus we understand that the grandmother and the Misfit have
equal importance in "A Good Man Is Hard to Find." One need
neither develop (as did one schoolteacher) a "real sentimental
attachment" for the Misfit nor regard him as a devil; similarly, the
grandmother remains precisely what we recognized her to be from
the start—a real woman, a member of the family. We last see her
sitting in a childlike posture and staring up at the sun. As far as her
lights would carry her, the grandmother was, as the Misfit recognizes, a good woman: "She would of been a good woman if it had
been somebody there to shoot her every minute of her life." To his
henchman's chortled response, "Some fun!" he says, "Shut up,
Bobbie Lee. It's no real pleasure in life" (p. 143).

In a sense, then, the Misfit has the last word. The reader's only
comfort so far as the Bailey family is concerned lies in their "good
manners"—the younger Mrs. Bailey is astonishingly polite—and in
the grandmother's recognition of her kinship with the killer. Her
reversion to a childlike posture and her staring at the sun suggest
that her death is a good one; furthermore, her death has prevented
resumption of her conflict between truth and survival. She has been
denied the false comforts of material subterfuge and is to join her
family in the woods where the Misfit's henchmen have thrown
their bodies. Whatever spiritual comfort may be drawn from a mass
murder Miss O'Connor has provided, and, seen quite apart from our
usual preoccupation with physical welfare, that comfort is considerable.

One should recall here that Miss O'Connor's concern is less to
provide comfort and "uplift," to use her word, than to actualize evil.
François Mauriac once said that his purpose was to provide a fictional
analogue to the Pascalian theme, "la misère de l'homme sans
Dieu."[4] With verve, Miss O'Connor realizes evil in this story, but at
the same time she makes it clear that any society which glorifies
the material may expect to find the Misfit lurking on the backroads,
demanding values other than monetary ones and seeking those

absolutes denied him by a society seeking only comfort and security.

To what extent does Miss O'Connor's collection fulfill the values traced in the dust of a Georgia backroad? The Misfit's preoccupations are eternal; his concern is less with legalistic justice than with divine justice. But do these stories merely reiterate the senselessness of evil and the fatuity of genteel virtue, with no hope for sinful man or his victims? Quite clearly, the Misfit finds no answer to his questions about Jesus, and he rejects the grandmother's gesture of kinship. Perhaps he recognizes that the gesture results from what Miss O'Connor once called the "haze of compassion," the humanist proclivity to pity which blurs moral distinctions, or perhaps he is aware that she identifies him with her son—he is wearing Bailey's shirt—and thus is still concerned only with the external. Nevertheless, the ideal represented by the Misfit's desire for truth is planted in the collection's opening story, and, like the seeds which open silently in young Tarwater's blood at the moment of his full awareness of grace, the ideal will grow throughout the collection and reach maturity in the final story. The progression is from the fact of evil and of sin toward the reality of atonement.

The central stories of the collection serve the doctrinal progression by reiterating the polar opposites which comprise man's nature; always capable of becoming a beast, man nevertheless retains his potential for full humanity and salvation. In the second story, "The River," Harry (Bevel) Ashfield is clearly saved: physically, he is saved from his terrible parents and from old Mr. Paradise, and spiritually, he is saved by his faith—childish though it is—in "the river of life." In "The Life You Save May Be Your Own" Mr. Shiftlet's callous abandoning of Lucynell Crater, "the angel of Gawd," whom he has married to get a car, contrasts sharply with his maudlin sentiment about his mother, whom he recalls as "a angel of Gawd." His shock at the youthful hitchhiker who says, "My old woman is a flea bag and yours is a stinking pole cat!" occasions his prayer that the Lord will "break forth and wash the slime from this earth." He races the turnip-shaped cloud toward Mobile as the story ends, and one suspects he will not get there. Like other O'Connor characters, he is enslaved by things; thus he imagines the soul to be like an automobile. His value is chiefly negative, for his goodness is nothing but pious mouthings.

Ruby Hill in "A Stroke of Good Fortune" provides a more positive value. Her realization of her unborn child as a force outside her "as if it were out nowhere in nothing, out nowhere, resting and waiting, with plenty of time" suggests her release from the purely physical and mortal concerns which obsess her at the story's opening. Her recognition of life is linked to awareness of death; her mind is on the eternal, not the temporal, when the story ends. Similarly, the child in "A Temple of the Holy Ghost," though she prays the Pharisee's prayer and "could never be a saint," renders holy in her own thought the sideshow freak who accepts his condition because "God made me thisaway and I don't dispute hit." Though the local preachers inspect the show and have the police close it down, the child's acceptance transcends their values, and the hermaphrodite's "testimony" is in her mind as the priest "raised the monstrance with the Host shining ivory-colored in the center of it."

A great part of Miss O'Connor's doctrinal meaning is expressed in "The Artificial Nigger," in which old Mr. Head's relationship with his grandson Nelson is restored only through the operation of mercy. The two, not speaking to one another, see a battered, agonized-looking statue of a Negro, and their wonder at it reunites them in a moment of communion: they look at "the artificial nigger" "as if they were faced with some great mystery, some monument to another's victory that brought them together in their common defeat." Afterward, "Mr. Head stood very still and felt the action of mercy touch him again but this time he knew that there were no words in the world that could name it. He understood that it grew out of agony, which is not denied to any man and which is given in strange ways to children. He understood it was all a man could carry into death to give his Maker and he suddenly burned with shame that he had so little of it to take with him" (p. 213).

In part, then, Miss O'Connor's point is that mercy, which grows out of agony, is all that one may take with him from this world. But Mr. Head's realization goes further: "He realized that he was forgiven for sins from the beginning of time, when he had conceived in his own heart the sin of Adam, until the present, when he had denied poor Nelson. He saw that no sin was too monstrous for him to claim as his own, and since God loved in proportion as He forgave, he felt ready at that instant to enter Paradise" (pp. 213–14).

Before he denied knowing Nelson, who looks exactly like him, Mr. Head "had been too good to deserve" mercy. His realization of the full extent of his need for mercy marks him as regenerate; he relies not upon himself and his virtues but upon a higher power.

In "A Circle in the Fire" Mrs. Cope proves as unable to handle the boys who visit her farm as Mr. Head was unable to guide Nelson successfully through the city. The face "of the new misery she felt" reveals that she cannot withstand the inexplicable evil of human nature, and her daughter realizes that her face "might have belonged to anybody, a Negro or a European." Agony erases differences.

"A Late Encounter with the Enemy" again underlines man's vanity and its futility in the light of eternal matters. Old 'General' Sash, whose chief memory has been the "preemy they had in Atlanta," had no use for history "because he never expected to meet it again." He and his granddaughter Sally Poker Sash are vain, but in different ways. She wants all the "upstarts who had turned the world on its head and unsettled the ways of decent living" to see her grandfather so they will know "what all was behind her." The old soldier's vanity is purely in himself, his uniform, and his "soword," given him by a movie public relations man named Govisky. His flight from history ends with the past and future converging in the present as he dies, and ironically, his Boy Scout attendant bumps the corpse out the back way to wait in "the long line at the Coca-Cola machine."

The next to last story brings the collection close to its thematic climax, for in "Good Country People" Joy (Hulga) Hopewell learns something of the nature of evil in losing her artificial leg, the tangible symbol of what she considers her "difference." At the same time she is rendered totally defenseless, both physically and emotionally. When Hulga consents to let Manley Pointer see how her artificial leg joins on, "it was like surrendering to him completely. It was like losing her own life and finding it again, miraculously, in his." But the story does not end here: Hulga learns that her "acquired disbelief" does not match her "lover's" natural depravity. In parting, with her glasses in his pocket and her artificial leg in his valise, he says, "you ain't so smart. I been believing in nothing since I was born!" As sensitive about her artificial leg as "a peacock about his tail," Hulga "took care of it as someone else would his soul, in private and almost with her own eyes turned away" (p. 261). Miss O'Connor said that the leg grows in importance every time it is mentioned and that when it is stolen, far more than a leg is stolen (*Mystery and Manners*, pp. 99–100).

If one has sought a good man in these stories, he has doubtless been disappointed: Red Sammy Butts spoke the truth in the scene at The Tower. "The Displaced Person" climaxes the collection by finally providing a good man and dramatizing the vicarious atonement. The story places the guilt for the death of the Savior squarely on the shoulders of sinful man, but it also extends the promise of grace: man's sin requires grace and, as Mr. Head realizes in "The Artificial Nigger," God loves in proportion as He forgives.

In "The Displaced Person" Mrs. McIntyre, her tenant farmer Mr. Shortley, and a Negro worker share equally in the guilt for Mr. Guizac's death, for Shortley was the agent of that death, permitting a tractor to run over the Polish refugee, and the others were accomplices. The Negro and Mrs. McIntyre had time to shout a warning, but instead, their eyes came "together in one look which froze them in collusion forever." Early in the story Mrs. McIntyre is the epitome of hardworking, respectable womanhood; she is a slightly younger, more prosperous version of the grandmother in the title story. After Guizac's death she declines rapidly: she loses her voice and her sight and, giving up the farm she has worked so hard to clear of debt, she retires to invalidism with no one but a priest to call on her.

Moving from the fact of evil to the fact of atonement, Miss O'Connor focuses her opening and closing stories on a similar character type. The character is hinted in other stories, notably in Mr. Head's false conviction of moral superiority, but the grandmother and Mrs. McIntyre are the most fully drawn examples of the type in this collection. Mrs. McIntyre sees herself as a totally virtuous victim of shiftless whites and lazy "niggers"; she preaches the secularist's doctrine to one old Negro when she says, "only the smart thrifty energetic ones are going to survive." She believes that everyone should have to struggle.

The grandmother in "A Good Man" is literally shot, but Mrs. McIntyre's first step toward becoming a truly "good woman," in the sense the Misfit meant, results from a figurative shot: her awareness of man's common guilt—hers as well as the shiftless, lazy people's —disables her physically, freeing her for spiritual consideration. Thus the Misfit's remark about the grandmother applies directly to Mrs.

McIntyre. Being shot every day of one's life is no comfortable way to exist, but by providing awareness of one's vulnerability, frailty, and guilt, it provides the ultimate hope. In Miss O'Connor's vision man's self-regard for his virtues, not his instinctive violence, frequently stands in his way of self-realization. In "Revelation," one of the stories in *Everything That Rises Must Converge,* this point is made explicit when Mrs. Turpin sees a vision of her kind loitering behind in the heavenly procession and realizes that their very virtues are being burned away.

Like Haze Motes, Mrs. McIntyre cannot see as long as she has physical sight, for it permits the things of this world to intervene; she cannot hear the doctrine taught her by the priest as long as she may interrupt with practical objections. She denies that she can be held responsible for the misery of the world, and her final judgment of Jesus is that He "was just another DP" (p. 294). The world, she thinks, is swelling up with people because people are selfish and have too many children. She gives lip service to religion though she knows none of it is true.

Neither moral responsibility nor religious commitment could have influenced Mrs. McIntyre to keep Mr. Guizac on her farm, but her avarice makes her rejoice in his hard work, for because of him she is able to displace other workers and save money. "That man's my salvation," she says at one point, but at the same time the foreigner's rigid movements, his lack of English and of racial prejudice, and his industry itself trouble her. She sees her way of life threatened. She has an excuse for dismissing the foreigner when she learns that he has been collecting money from a "dimwitted nigger" to bring his young cousin to America; in return, he has promised the Negro he may marry the girl. Guizac cannot understand Mrs. McIntyre's emotional reaction to this arrangement, for, as he says, "She no care he black. She been in camp." His employer, unfortunately, cannot appreciate the meaning of being in camp, nor can she understand a man who calls himself a Christian being willing to "bring a poor innocent girl over here and marry her to something like that."

Just as Mrs. McIntyre's collusion in Guizac's death leads to the action of grace, so does the spiteful Mrs. Shortley's hatred of Guizac lead to a happy end for her—spiritually, if not physically. Overhearing Mrs. McIntyre's plans to fire Shortley, the woman packs her family's goods and leaves the farm. She associates Guizac with the pope and the devil, and she is outraged at being displaced by a DP. Before she can tell her husband where she wants him to drive the family car, Mrs. Shortley dies, but her eyes open on the "immense frontiers of her true country." The implication is that her ignorance, hatred, and outrage combine to save her through the mysterious workings of grace.

In *The True Country: Themes in the Fiction of Flannery O'Connor*, Carter W. Martin fails to quote the words about Mrs. Shortley's eyes opening on "the immense frontiers of her true country," though he quotes almost the entire description of what he regards as her ironically humorous death. He observes accurately the irony that Mrs. Shortley's death "is presented in the very images which she had associated with Mr. Guizac,"[5] but his desire to render her death grotesque and unregenerate leads to his omission of the very phrase from which he drew his title. Martin apparently regards Mrs. Shortley's ignorance as adequate cause for damnation; on the contrary, Miss O'Connor makes her salvation explicit.

Ironically, Guizac is finally made to suffer for Mrs. Shortley's death. Shortley returns, determined that Guizac killed his wife, and even convinces Mrs. McIntyre that she "owes" him reinstatement in his former job. He talks with newfound volubility to everyone, presenting his case in illogical terms which are never questioned. Minimizing the difference between the first and second world wars and eradicating the difference between Poles and Germans, he argues for Guizac's dismissal: " 'All men was created free and equal,' he said to Mrs. McIntyre, 'and I risked my life and limb to prove it. Gone over there and fought and bled and died and come back on over here and find out who's got my job—just exactly who I been fighting. It was a hand-grenade come that near to killing me and I seen who throwed it—little man with eye-glasses just like his. Might have bought them at the same store. Small world,' and he gave a bitter little laugh" (p. 296). The glasses Shortley mentions frequently are the only gold-rimmed glasses in this story; they differentiate Guizac as does his unreformed religion. Eventually Mrs. McIntyre begins "to understand that she had a moral obligation to fire the Pole," but she puts it off until it is too late. Shortley leaves the tractor on an incline and it rolls over Guizac's body.

In addition to linking Guizac to Christ through Mrs. McIntyre's statements that Guizac has upset the balance of the farm and that "Christ was just another DP," Miss O'Connor advances that association through two important symbols. The first is the peacock, which Father Flynn admires and associates with the transfiguration; the sight of the peacock leads him to say, "He came to atone for our sins," in response to Mrs. McIntyre's statement that Guizac didn't have to come. Like the priest, old Astor, the Negro workman, admires the peacock; he carries corn in his pocket to make the bird follow him. Mrs. Shortley, who needs no such lure, scorns the priest's "foolishness" over the bird just as she scorns Guizac's "unreformed religion." She apparently does not need the symbolic magnificence of the bird any more than she needs the sacramental ministration of the Church.

The peacock is also important in other ways. Mrs. McIntyre has been married three times, but only her first husband, a judge, is dead. She hates the peacocks and intends to let them die out, but she fears to destroy them because they belonged to the judge (who had kept them because they made him feel rich), and she has "a super-stitious fear of annoying [him] in his grave." She scorns the priest's admiration of the birds, for she sees no beauty or symbolism in their multiple-eyed tails. Fear prevents her open denial of religion, much less Christianity, but she is embarrassed by religious talk, which she considers impractical. She intends to let it die out with the peacocks.

The judge's values lead to the other symbol, a statue which he treasured as highly as his peacocks. Despite the apparent prosperity of Mrs. McIntyre's few years as the judge's wife and the rumors of his wealth, he left her little more than a mortgage-ridden farm with the timber freshly cut, the peacocks, and a statue to mark his grave. He had bought the statue, a naked angel, partly because it reminded him of is wife and partly because he wanted a genuine work of art over his grave. Though the judge was apparently a fraud, his widow continues to revere him through two additional and unhappy marriages; she holds onto the farm and tolerates the peacocks. In the meantime, however, the statue has been stolen by covetous tenants who knocked it down with an ax, leaving only the toes. Until it was stolen, Mrs. McIntyre had regarded the statue as hideous. The essential emptiness of her values is epitomized by her perverse reverence for the judge: she keeps his office intact with its locked but empty safe at the center. Similarly, the ravished statue symbolizes her spiritual need: the tenants, for all their shiftlessness, knew enough to value the angel and were willing to use violence to obtain it. Anagogically, Mrs. McIntyre's plight is clear. Her "angel" is taken away and her peacocks are dying out; all that remains for her is the common legacy, the terms of judgment after the fall, but the necessity to work to keep the farm blinds her to transcendent values.

The purpose of the Displaced Person is perhaps to replace the "angel" in Mrs. McIntyre's life and to restore the peacocks' meaning before the last bird dies. Until this purpose is achieved, however, Mrs. McIntyre's change of attitude toward the stolen statue marks a slight gain, just as Nelson and Mr. Head's common racial arrogance serves the cause of mercy in "The Artificial Nigger." The violent theft of the angel serves also as precursor to the central themes of the two novels, a point which emphasizes again the unity of Miss O'Connor's fiction.

Like Hulga in "Good Country People," Mrs. McIntyre conspires with evil, and her knowledge of her collusion in Guizac's death leaves her defenseless. Mrs. McIntyre loses her sight and voice, for those physical powers stand in the way of her redemption; Hulga loses the artificial leg, for the danger to her soul lies not in a fleshly limb or in her senses but in the symbol of her deprivation and difference. After all those years of struggle with her "help," Mrs. McIntyre, left blind, dumb, and alone, "hardly noticed that she had no help left."

Haze Motes, attempting to establish a comfortable, tranquil church at peace, a Church Without Christ, preached that "there was no Fall because there was nothing to fall from, and no Redemption because there was no Fall and no Judgment because there wasn't the first two. Nothing matters but that Jesus was a liar." Though one of her faults is that she would never admit it, Mrs. McIntyre advocates Haze's doctrine; she is a pillar of the secular society, one of the "smart thrifty energetic ones [who] are going to survive." Haze's repudiation leads finally to acceptance; his rejection of the bloodless mummy marks the beginning of a purely spiritual pilgrimage in which he is no longer hampered by secular substitutes. Mrs. McIntyre has more than a "new jesus" to lose before she may begin to gain, but the desecrated angel over the judge's grave symbolizes her need. Furthermore, both Haze and Mrs. McIntyre must finally lose their eyes before they can attain true sight.

Miss O'Connor's repeated paradox, admittedly alien to the contemporary mind, is simply that one must lose his life to find it. The quest in *A Good Man Is Hard to Find* begins at the Tower of Babel, but it ends at Golgotha; goodness is redefined between the first and last stories, and Guizac has meaning in terms of the Misfit's claim that Jesus "thown everything off balance" just as much as in Mrs. McIntyre's self-seeking reproach that the DP is "extra." The meaning of the collection is this: human nature is such that Christ must continue to bring the sword of divisiveness; a good man such as Guizac is as unlikely to "fit in" as Jesus is, for the good man makes intolerable the effort to avoid judgment through denial of the fall and of redemption.

CHAPTER FIVE

A Second Novel & Related Stories

"From the Days of John the Baptist until Now"

THE VIOLENT BEAR IT AWAY appeared in 1960, but it had been in the working stage as early as 1953, when Miss O'Connor wrote to Robert Fitzgerald that she had a "nice gangster" in her new novel. As Fitzgerald observes in the introduction to *Everything That Rises Must Converge* (p. xxi), Rufus Florida Johnson disappeared from the novel and "turned up a long time later" in another story, "The Lame Shall Enter First" (*Sewanee Review* [Summer 1962]). Two works published in 1955 are also directly related to *The Violent Bear It Away*: "You Can't Be Poorer than Dead" (*New World Writing*) and "The Artificial Nigger" (*Kenyon Review* [Spring 1955]). The latter story doubtless helped Miss O'Connor clarify the characters of old Mason Tarwater and Francis Marion Tarwater; they appeared in "The Artificial Nigger" as Mr. Head and his grandson Nelson. Appropriately, Mr. Head's denial of his grandson suggests St. Peter's denial of Christ, and the old man's name was altered for the novel to suggest the petrine quality: a mason is a builder with stone.

The trip to Atlanta which provides the action of "The Artificial Nigger" is not dramatized in the novel, but Francis Marion Tarwater recalls a trip to the city with his great-uncle, whom the boy takes to task for failing to testify to the city-dwellers. "The Artificial Nigger" is a story of ritual initiation; Mr. Head wishes to teach his grandson a lesson, to show him the evils of the city so he will never wish to go there again. Ironically, the old man learns a great deal about himself as a result of the experience: he learns the extent of his own sinfulness and is brought to recognize his own need for mercy. In *The*

Violent Bear It Away young Tarwater's life in the city with his uncle Rayber dramatizes again a common fate shared by an old man and a boy. Miss O'Connor's awareness of Rayber's importance in *The Violent Bear It Away* is suggested by her correspondence with Fitzgerald in 1959 about her reworking of Rayber's character, which she said had been "the trouble all along."

The "nice gangster" who originally appeared in *The Violent Bear It Away* is analogous to Francis Marion Tarwater who took his place. Even the three-part names are suggestive of this evolution: Rufus Florida Johnson and Francis Marion Tarwater. When Rufus reappears in "The Lame Shall Enter First," his relationship to Sheppard, the do-gooder recreation director, is comparable to young Tarwater's relationship to the secularist schoolteacher, Rayber. The creative process of writing her second novel involved Miss O'Connor's differentiation of characters and focusing on one of several possible relationships, including grandfather-grandson ("The Artificial Nigger"), uncle-nephew (*The Violent Bear It Away*), and social worker–delinquent ("The Lame Shall Enter First"). *The Violent Bear It Away* achieves the values of all three sets of relationships, for old Mason Tarwater is uncle to Rayber and great-uncle to Francis, while Rayber is both uncle and social worker to the incipiently violent and delinquent young Tarwater. Similarities in *The Violent Bear It Away* and "The Lame Shall Enter First" will require lengthy comparisons of content and character. In some ways the meaning of the story illuminates the meaning of the novel, but the nature of Miss O'Connor's fiction is such that the novel becomes more broadly comprehensible if first viewed in its relationship to the works which preceded it.

In particular, *Wise Blood* and Miss O'Connor's attitudes about it ten years after its publication serve to inform the critic of correct approaches to the later novel. In a brief introductory note to *Wise Blood* in the Signet edition, 3 *by Flannery O'Connor,* the author made clear her *donnée,* or, as she put it, her "preoccupations": *"Wise Blood* was written by an author congenitally innocent of theory, but one with certain preoccupations. That belief in Christ is to some a matter of life and death has been a stumbling block for readers who would prefer to think it a matter of no great consequence." In light of this statement, Miss O'Connor's earlier insistence in the same note that *Wise Blood* is a "comic novel about a Christian *malgré lui,* and as such very serious, for all comic novels that are any good must be written about matters of life and death" takes on new meaning. Although it is admittedly a funny novel, *Wise Blood* is comic fundamentally because it ends happily with Haze Motes's total surrender to belief.

The Violent Bear It Away is also a novel about a Christian (or Christians) *malgré lui;* furthermore, Miss O'Connor's preoccupation with the distinction between physical and spiritual vision, so basic to *Wise Blood,* carries over into the second novel, as does the conflict within man's dual nature. Her note to *Wise Blood* makes a valuable comment on this aspect of both novels: her acknowledgment there that "free will does not mean one will, but many wills conflicting in one man" supports this study's reading of *Wise Blood,* which sees Enoch Emery as the embodiment of man's animal nature, happily escaped by Haze Motes through repudiation of the false prophets Asa Hawks, Onnie Jay Holy, and Solace Layfield. All these characters represent aspects of man's entrapment by the physical, the secular, and the material. Layfield, Haze's "double," is the sacrificial victim whose death sets Haze free to testify.

Francis Marion Tarwater, like Haze Motes, passes from a desire not to believe, through a violent attempt at repudiation, and finally into a ritualistic cleansing which leads to an acceptance as violent as his former denial. *The Violent Bear It Away* opens with an epigraph from the Gospel:

> From the days of John the Baptist until now, the Kingdom of Heaven suffereth violence, and the violent bear it away.
> St. Matthew, 11:12

The epigraph has troubled most critics who wish (as they did with *Wise Blood*) to regard belief in Christ as a "matter of no great consequence," certainly not as a "matter of life and death." Stanley Edgar Hyman, for instance, in his Minnesota pamphlet *Flannery O'Connor,* interprets the epigraph as follows: "Its clear meaning is that the violent are enemies of the Kingdom, capturing it from the righteous, as a sign of the imminent coming of the Messiah, the Christ. In this sense, the Tarwaters are mad fanatics carrying away the Kingdom from its lukewarm heirs, and Rayber is an equally mad fanatic preaching secular salvation. . . . The effect of the novel's action on young Tarwater is to extirpate the rational self. . . , to burn away all reason and leave him entirely violent and mad" (p. 24). Hyman's reading does not take into account the possibility that "suffereth" also means "permits," as in the familiar New Testament passage beginning "Suffer the little children." Nor does it suggest Miss O'Connor's approval of the fanaticism and madness, if such descriptions be appropriate, of her backwoods fundamentalists. "Old Tarwater," said Miss O'Connor, "is the hero of *The Violent Bear It Away,* and I'm right behind him one hundred percent."[1]

Although the epigraph to the novel may be ambiguous, there are two other relevant passages from the Bible which permit no doubt as to the book's basic meaning. They are 1 Peter 5:8 and 1 Kings 13.

In 1 Peter, the apostle warns "the strangers scattered throughout Pontus, Galatin, Cappodocia, Asia, and Bithynia" to "be sober, be vigilant," for their "adversary the devil, as a roaring lion, walketh about seeking whom he may devour." Like Peter, old Mason Tarwater issues a warning to Francis: "You are the kind of boy that the devil is always going to be offering to assist, to give you a smoke or a drink or a ride, and to ask you your bidnis [*sic*]" (p. 337). In the course of the novel Francis takes the advice of his "friend," at first a projection of himself and later a separate entity, who turns out, at last, to be his "adversary," and is so named in the last few pages of the novel. The violet eyes of the "friend" are duplicated in the colors associated with the homosexual who picks Francis up, learns his "bidnis," gives him a doped cigarette and drink, takes him to the woods, and rapes him. When the homosexual emerged from the woods, "his delicate skin had acquired a faint pink tint as if he had refreshed himself on blood" (p. 441). Not only is the parallel with Peter exact, but it exactly fulfills old Mason's prophecy, for he had also told Francis to "beware the lion of the Lord set in the path of the false prophet" (p. 317). Peter's injunctions to the early Christians included putting away all fleshly excesses and "abominable idolatries." When Francis is raped, he has in his possession a corkscrew given him by Rayber; he boasts to the homosexual, "This here thing will open anything." Appropriately, he uses the corkscrew to open the doped liquor; equally appropriately, the homosexual steals the corkscrew (a gift of his secular uncle) and his hat (a vestige of his old life) and leaves him naked. (The new clothes piled beside him, also a gift from Rayber, are worn only because he has no others.)

The application of 1 Peter to Miss O'Connor's novel is made even more relevant by the name Mason Tarwater. The critics have generally noted that old Mason is similar to John the Baptist, but they have not related him to Saint Peter through the meaning of his first name. A mason builds with stone; thus Mason Tarwater's fundamentalism is a reminder of the petrine basis of faith. The name Tarwater calls attention to the cleansing, purgative power of water, for *tar* (as a verb) means "urge to action," and *tarwater,* as Hyman notes, is a "discredited folk cure-all" (*Flannery O'Connor,* p. 20). (The question may be, discredited by whom?)

The New Testament is the fulfillment of the Old, and Miss O'Connor has drawn Mason Tarwater's prophecy in part from 1 Kings 13. Mason himself, in his role as John the Baptist, stands as the last prophet of the Old Dispensation and the first martyr of the New; hence it is suitable that he echo an Old Testament passage. In 1 Kings an unnamed man of the Lord predicts the destruction of King Jeroboam's altar at Bethel because of the king's desecration of it. To prove he is a true prophet, the unnamed man withers Jeroboam's hand. Obeying God's commandment, he refuses to eat or drink with Jeroboam, but before he leaves the idolatrous country, a local prophet seduces him into eating. Afterward the local prophet, an old man, pronounces judgment: "Thy carcass shall not come unto the sepulchre of thy fathers." Shortly thereafter the man of the Lord is killed by a lion but his flesh is not devoured; the lion watches by his body until the old prophet comes for it and buries it in his own sepulchre.

Miss O'Connor's intentions and execution here are obvious. When he kidnaps Francis, Mason Tarwater leaves a note for his nephew Rayber saying that the prophet he will raise out of the boy will burn Rayber's eyes clean. Later, encouraged by his wife, a welfare worker, Rayber goes to Powderhead to reclaim the boy but is repulsed by Mason's shotgun fire. He is deafened by one blast and thereafter wears a hearing aid attached to his glasses. When Mason dies, Francis goes to Rayber's house in the city but disdains his uncle's food; he enjoys nothing he eats and hardly touches food until he arrives at Cherokee Lodge, where he gorges himself until he throws up.

Shortly thereafter (at the end of part two) he drowns Rayber's son Bishop, and the effect of that drowning is to alter Rayber totally: his eyes have been burned clean. Armed with Rayber's gift, the corkscrew, Francis sets out for Powderhead, but he uses the corkscrew to open the doped liquor and is "devoured" by the "lion . . . set in the path of the false prophet." When he awakes, violated, robbed, and naked, his eyes "looked as if, touched with a coal like the lips of the prophet, they would never be used for ordinary sights again" (p. 442). The shocking metaphor of the descent of divine power, prepared for in part one with the sexual implications of the effect of Francis's first drink of liquor, leads to his spiritual rebirth.

Only the final revelation remains for Francis: when he discovers that he has not cremated Mason at all, he has a vision of his dead uncle with the multitude feeding on the multiplied loaves and fishes. He realizes at last that his hunger is such that no food on earth can satisfy it. Despite the clarity of Miss O'Connor's intent, Stuart L. Burns sees Tarwater's acceptance of his true prophetic role as a result of his "failure to achieve selfhood independent of his great-uncle's influence." Consequently, Tarwater's "assumption of the prophet's role is outlined in terms of surrender rather than achievement"; Burns sees this assumption as "grotesque."[2] Burns's reading disregards the prophetic nature of the novel, based as it is upon scriptural sources and structured in such a way as to dramatize the ultimate distinction between old Tarwater's mission to tell of God's justice and the boy's mission to tell of His mercy.

Though great parts of the novel remain to be examined, the application of the scriptural sources establishes that Francis Marion Tarwater, far from being abandoned to the madness of fanaticism or surrendering compulsively to the distorting influence of his great-uncle, realizes a destiny sanctioned by the prophets: if his eyes will not see normal sights again, his compensation is grace. To complete the cycle, young Tarwater sets out for the city as the book ends; his great-uncle had preached the "terrible speed of God's justice," and Francis's mission is to "GO WARN THE CHILDREN OF GOD OF THE TERRIBLE SPEED OF MERCY." The emphasis on God's mercy recalls the conclusion of "The Artificial Nigger."

The action of *The Violent Bear It Away* requires a full week, and the scene shifts from Powderhead to the city and, finally, back to

Powderhead. The structure is almost identical to that of *Wise Blood*, for Rayber, who is introduced in part two, is left at the end of the section very much as Enoch Emery is left at the end of the second section of the first novel. Furthermore, as in *Wise Blood*, part two provides the basis for the reversal which occurs in the concluding section. To emphasize this movement, Miss O'Connor numbers the three parts, but the chapters run consecutively from start to finish, thus interlocking the parts.

Briefly, part one (in addition to providing backgrounds, as must all three sections in this highly telescoped book) initiates Francis's conflict, which is almost totally internal. As he prepares to carry out his great-uncle's commission to bury him, a "strange voice" emerges to express unwillingness to dig the grave; later the voice materializes into a "friend" who accompanies and advises him throughout the novel. The "friend" encourages him to doubt what his uncle has taught him and taunts him into getting drunk without completing the grave. Setting fire to his uncle's house, where he thinks old Mason's body remains, Francis rushes into the night and to his first encounter, alone, with the world. The reader has known from the novel's first sentence that Mason's body received Christian burial at the hands of a neighboring Negro, but the boy leaves Powderhead certain his defiance has been effective: old Tarwater had feared cremation at the hands of his other nephew, Rayber, and had warned Francis to "beware the lion of the Lord set in the path of the false prophet" if he permitted Rayber to cremate his body. Picked up by a salesman who wishes to use him as an assistant, Francis gets to the city, and a significant structural clue occurs just as he arrives: waking from a nap, he sees the city lights and thinks he is seeing the flames he left behind him. (The action will be cyclical, returning to Powderhead.) Despite his will to the contrary, Francis is dropped at his uncle Rayber's house. (Had it not been for Mason's kidnapping him, Francis would have grown up with Rayber, for, as he is proud to relate, he was "born at a wreck" and his parents are dead. He is the illegitimate son of Rayber's sister, the product of an affair Rayber engineered.)

Francis is convinced not only that he has avoided performing the first mission imposed upon him by Mason Tarwater but also that he can resist the second—the baptism of Rayber's idiot son, Bishop. (Old

Tarwater had tried on numerous occasions to baptize the child, but Rayber had always thwarted him; years earlier, Mason had kidnapped Rayber and baptized him, just as he later baptized Francis despite Rayber's objections.) Part two of the novel, occurring largely in the city, dramatizes Francis's compulsion to baptize Bishop and his efforts to resist that compulsion. Large parts of this section focus on Rayber and permit him to voice his secularist arguments in behalf of "freedom." Ironically, he is far from free, though he thinks he has controlled his fanaticism imbued from Mason; he limits his experience rigidly to prevent the old madness from recurring. Rayber honestly seeks to understand Francis and to make friends with him; with Bishop, the two walk interminably, seeing museums, parks, and other sights of the city. Despite Rayber's best efforts, he and Francis are increasingly estranged, partly as a result of Francis's strange interest in Bishop.

Eventually, at Cherokee Lodge where Rayber takes the two boys for an outing, Francis drowns Bishop to prove to Rayber that he can act and to prove to himself that he will not baptize the boy. His "friend," of course, encourages him to do the act and officiates over the violence: "Don't you have to do something at last, one thing to prove you ain't going to do another?" (p. 402). Just before the drowning, Rayber, intending to illustrate free will to Francis, had resorted to an appeal to determinism: certain laws, he argued, govern what all men do, and Francis is no different. Francis's response was "Wait and see" (p. 418). Rayber had once tried to drown his son and failed only because he suddenly thought he could not live without the boy; Francis Tarwater succeeds, but, like his uncle, he fails in his purpose: at the moment of victory, having done one thing to prove he would not do the other, he says the formula of baptism. In his room, at the moment of the murder, Rayber awakes to a terrible stillness and then claws at his hearing aid, which makes the bellows of the drowning son seem to be torn from inside the father, as if something were tearing itself free. Rayber instinctively knows that Francis has baptized Bishop even as he drowned him and is setting off into the darkness for an encounter with his fate. Rayber prepares himself to overcome the pain he knows is his due and collapses only when he realizes that it will not come.

Part three is devoted to Francis's return to Powderhead, a name which by now certainly requires no interpretation. He catches a ride with a truckdriver, similar in some ways to the traveling salesman of part one. Unable to think or talk about anything but otherworldly matters, Francis fails to satisfy the driver's request for jokes; like Bevel Summers in "The River," Francis looks as if he does not know what a joke is. The driver gives Francis a sandwich which the boy cannot eat, and they stop the truck to sleep. In a dream Francis reenacts his baptismal drowning of Bishop. His cry of the baptismal formula wakes him; he then wakes the driver, who puts him out of the truck. The "monster" roars past him, and he continues walking.

Hungry and thirsty, Francis gives his sandwich to a Negro child in return for water from a well. In the water he sees a reflection, probably his "friend's," which frightens him. The water does not satisfy him and he begins to long for a "purple drink," which he plans to buy at a grocery near Powderhead. The proprietress, looking like a gigantic angel, refuses to serve him and scolds him for burning his uncle's house. Finally he gets another ride, this time with a vaguely familiar looking man with lavender eyes, driving a lavender car and wearing a lavender shirt. We recall the description of Francis's "friend" at the drowning: his eyes were violet, intense, and hungry. Smoking a doped cigarette, Francis opens the stranger's doped liquor with the corkscrew, and old Mason's prophecy is all but fulfilled. The rape is not dramatized, but its effects on Francis are to scorch his eyes and to prepare him for the final revelation.

Part three begins at night and its action requires the remainder of that night, all the next day, and part of the next night. At the end of the book it is night again as Francis sets out for the city, fully aware at last of his mission. He burns the spot where he had been violated and, rushing to the road, discovers that "it was the home road, ground that had been familiar to him since his infancy but now . . . looked like strange and alien country" (p. 442). Advancing toward his former home, he burns the woods, his material legacy, and places a wall of fire between himself and his "friend," whom he finally recognizes as his "adversary." With that realization Miss O'Connor achieves her dramatic resolution of conflict; Francis recognizes his bestial nature, that part of man guided by the archfiend, and severs himself from it.

At the end of her book Miss O'Connor makes explicit several

points. After Francis realizes he has failed to cremate Mason Tarwater, he has a vision of the multitude feeding upon the multiplied loaves and fishes, a thought which had once repulsed him. He sees his uncle waiting to be fed, and suddenly his own hunger ceases to be a pain and becomes a tide: "He felt it rising in himself through time and darkness, rising through the centuries, and he knew that it rose in a line of men whose lives were chosen to sustain it, who would wander in the world, strangers from that violent country where the silence is never broken except to shout the truth. He felt it building from the blood of Abel to his own, rising and engulfing him" (p. 446).

Feeling the tide lifting and turning him, Francis whirls toward the line of trees, Miss O'Connor's ubiquitous image of revelation. There, in an image almost precisely like the one seen by O. E. Parker at the climax of the brilliant later story "Parker's Back," Francis sees his final sign: "Rising and spreading in the night, a red-gold tree of fire ascended as if it would consume the darkness in one tremendous burst of flame. He knew that this was the fire that had encircled Daniel, that had raised Elijah from the earth, that had spoken to Moses and would in an instant speak to him." He throws himself to the ground and hears, at last, the command: "GO WARN THE CHILDREN OF GOD OF THE TERRIBLE SPEED OF MERCY. The words were as silent as seeds opening one at a time in his blood" (p. 447).

With the vigor and majesty of an Old Testament vision, Miss O'Connor has dramatized the birth of a prophet who is the culmination of the Old and the New Dispensations. Francis's experience is at one with mankind's experience; the tide rises in him "from the blood of Abel," the first biblical sacrifice to man's innate evil. The fire he sets to exorcise his devil is the same flame with which Daniel, Elijah, and Moses communed; henceforth he is a wanderer.

The man of the Lord in 1 Kings 13, though prophetically "true," is punished for breaking God's commandment. The Lord's lion kills him and his carcass is not returned to his father's sepulchre. Similarly, Francis Marion Tarwater's old self is killed by the lion (his "friend"), and the new self is alienated from earthly concerns. His rebirth is clearly symbolized: he awakes naked and lacking his hat and his corkscrew, vestiges of his previous identity. His burned eyes see a "strange and alien country," though it is the home road he walks.

Just as the early Christians were a "peculiar people," so Tarwater is alien and homeless; the biblical parallel suggests that, like the New Testament Christians, he will evangelize the Gentiles, never returning to an earthly home, not even for burial.

The Violent Bear It Away is clearly Miss O'Connor's greatest single accomplishment, but so richly is it compacted with symbols which function both intrinsically and allusively that it continues to be misunderstood. The argument that it is a book chiefly, or exclusively, about the vocation of the priesthood leaves Rayber's story unsatisfactorily resolved. The argument that it is about madness is simply untenable except in the sense that the world always sees eternal vision as madness. A more judicious interpretation is that both Francis and Rayber are finally brought through the operations of mercy and of grace to the salvation neither of them seeks and both attempt to deny. This argument may be advanced best by dealing with the novel as it relates to Miss O'Connor's later short story "The Lame Shall Enter First."

The Violent and the Lame

Almost ten years elapsed between Flannery O'Connor's initial creation of the character Rufus Florida Johnson, originally intended as the hero of *The Violent Bear It Away,* and his appearance in her story "The Lame Shall Enter First." When the novel appeared in 1960, there was scarcely a trace left of Rufus; nevertheless, his basic plight—the plight of the fundamentalist confronted with secularist do-gooders—continued to interest Miss O'Connor, and it was inevitable that the "nice gangster" would return to her work. Rufus's exclusion from the novel probably resulted in part from Miss O'Connor's discovery of the value of establishing avuncular relations among the major characters in *The Violent Bear It Away.* "The Lame Shall Enter First," on the other hand, clearly requires a gangster type, a delinquent, whom the ironically named Sheppard, a social worker, may attempt to "father." Rufus's rejection of the secular paternalism expressed by Sheppard leads to the social worker's realization of the failure of his relationship to his real son. In *The Violent Bear It Away* young Tarwater has a choice of two uncles, the fundamentalist prophet and the secularist schoolteacher; in "The

Lame Shall Enter First" the secularist schoolteacher's counterpart has his choice between his greedy, dull-witted son and the bright, fundamentalist delinquent. He makes the wrong choice, for his love is self-seeking, like Rayber's love for his idiot son. When Sheppard recoils from what he sees as the evil of Rufus, he is left with no earthly comfort, for, like Rayber, he has lost the object which motivates and contains his selfish love.

The connections between "The Lame Shall Enter First" and *The Violent Bear It Away* have been apparent to most of Miss O'Connor's critics, but those connections have not been observed as thematic and pervasive so much as incidental. Though Robert Fitzgerald recognizes that Rufus Florida Johnson drops out of the novel to reappear in the short story, he does not suggest the ways in which Miss O'Connor doubtless considered Francis Tarwater's relationship to his uncle Rayber as analogous to Rufus's relationship to Sheppard. As a matter of fact, for all his appreciation of Miss O'Connor's work, Fitzgerald misses the point of "The Lame Shall Enter First." Stanley Edgar Hyman has called attention to part of Fitzgerald's misreading of that story.

In brief, Fitzgerald's error is to assume (at an important juncture in the story) that Miss O'Connor meant what her character Sheppard thought; ironically, Fitzgerald's mistaking her technique places him with the "deaf, dumb, and blind" readers for whom she said the writer who believes in "religious realities" must provide "desperate answers." His error is particularly unfortunate in that it appears in the introduction to the collection containing the story and will doubtless be given the stamp of authority.

Toward the end of "The Lame Shall Enter First" Miss O'Connor wrote that Sheppard "saw the clear-eyed Devil, the sounder of hearts, leering at him from the eyes of Johnson." In his introduction Fitzgerald dismisses the complexity of this story by coupling it with "The Comforts of Home" and saying that "brainless and brainy depravity are enough to . . . bring down in ruin" the central characters in both stories (p. xxxi). Hyman recognizes that Sheppard, not Miss O'Connor, sees Rufus as the Devil: "Miss O'Connor's own reading, I believe, is consistent with her radical Christian dualism and far more challenging: not Rufus but Sheppard is the type of Satan, taking over God's prerogatives in His assumed absence; and Rufus is the true prophetic voice of judgment, saying of Sheppard 'He thinks he's Jesus Christ!' and challenging him, 'Satan has you in his power'" (*Flannery O'Connor*, p. 26).

Hyman's reading here is the better one, but unfortunately he has not worked out his argument satisfactorily either, for within a few pages he writes that Johnson "succeeds in converting Norton (Sheppard's son) to Satanism (and thus to suicide) since, as Sheppard recognizes (in the story's central irony) but cannot understand, 'the boy would rather be in hell than nowhere'" (p. 35). The problems in Hyman's interpretation are largely the results of his failure to grasp the author's position in the story and how it controls her use of narrative and symbolic techniques. In part his failure is inconsistency: how can Rufus at once serve as "the true prophetic voice of judgment" and as the tempter who converts Norton to Satanism? (Furthermore, Hyman apparently equates Harry Ashfield's suicide—committed in full belief in a heavenly salvation—with Satanism, but this argument is clearly untenable.) Norton is a child, and his belief in Rufus's "otherworldly" alternative to Sheppard's secularism is so intense that, though one may judge the child misguided, one cannot in good faith judge him a Satan-worshipper. Hyman also speaks of the "central irony" of Sheppard's realizing Norton would rather be in hell than nowhere, but the story actually states that Sheppard realizes the boy would rather his mother be in hell than nowhere. Even granting that Norton himself would make the same choice, Hyman has forgotten that Norton and Rufus take precautions to assure Norton's salvation: when a Bible must be stolen, Rufus steals it in order that the child not jeopardize his chances of heavenly reunion with his mother. Rufus and Norton believe that the late Mrs. Sheppard is surely enjoying bliss because she believed in Jesus and was not a whore.

Actually neither Rufus nor Sheppard is the "type of Satan," and the story's theme has more to do with salvation than with damnation. Norton's conversion is to the childlike (therefore blessed) faith of Harry Ashfield; the instruments of his salvation are a secularist father, a fanatical hoodlum, and a "slender channel to the stars"—a telescope purchased by Sheppard as a means of appealing to the intellect of his juvenile delinquent charge, whom he wished "to develop" to feed his own ego. The symbols of the story are almost precisely those of the novel. The corkscrew bought as a "peace offering" for Francis Tarwater opens the "fatal" (in a purely metaphorical sense) bottle of liquor; once young Tarwater has drunk the devil's liquor, he is defenseless, and his physical assault leads to his spiritual rebirth. Similarly, the telescope, though intended to help dissipate Rufus's superstition and his antipathy to space travel, actually serves to enforce Norton's belief in heaven and in his mother's spiritual salvation. There are few more touching passages in contemporary literature than the one in which Norton waves exultantly toward the sky, where he thinks he has found his mother. Just as the mystery of grace subverts the corkscrew and Tarwater's faith in it, so also does grace manipulate the telescope and the events of "The Lame Shall Enter First" to provide a happy spiritual ending for all the characters.

It will be recalled that in *The Violent Bear It Away* Rayber gives young Tarwater two alternatives—to give in to his compulsion or to overcome it and be born again in what Rayber prefers to consider "the natural way," through his own efforts. Sheppard provides precisely the same alternatives to Norton: he can offer his son no spiritual hope; instead he asks the boy to accept the bleak fact of death and the tawdry idea of immortality through one's goodness living on in those he loves. Norton is apparently little comforted by these "choices." What Rufus has to offer—the age-old and ever-dramatic conflict between God and Satan, Good and Evil—appeals to his imagination as his father's dry, mechanical goodness cannot.

Rayber's choices drive Francis to his drowning of Bishop, and Sheppard's choices lead to Norton's hanging himself. It will be seen that Rayber's loss of Bishop deprives him of all that stands between him and reversion to fanaticism—the longing to see the impossible visions his great-uncle Mason had seen with his "fish-colored madman's eyes." Similarly, Sheppard, stripped of his sense of infallibility and the messianic compulsion to "save" the world through acts of secular charity, achieves self-knowledge, which is a form of grace.

As Miss O'Connor counts spiritual gains, Sheppard's ability to see the Devil leering at him from Rufus's eyes is a great gain, for he has earlier denied the existence of Satan, as well as God and Jesus. He is convinced that Rufus lies and steals to compensate for his deformity, his gross clubfoot, which Sheppard hopes to cover in a new shoe.

(What better modern parallel of the purse and the sow's ear?) Rufus maintains throughout that he is wicked not because of his clubfoot but because Satan has him in his power, and it becomes increasingly clear that his wickedness is not self-interested: it is not the usual sort of evil. Not all evil, Sheppard must learn, is of the sort that may be prevented by offering the transgressor a greater advantage for doing good; not all evil results from deprivation, either intellectual or physical, and not all evil may be prevented by teaching a boy to look through a telescope or by giving him a new shoe for his deformed foot. (Miss O'Connor strikes a glancing blow at Father Flanagan of Boys Town fame in one of her earliest stories, "The Capture," in which her child character, whose values are wholly secular, considers starting a home for boys; one immediately thinks of Bing Crosby's portrayal of the man who believed "there's no such thing as a bad boy." Miss O'Connor would have us believe otherwise.)

Sheppard, the enlightened secularist, has protected his son from the false hopes of religious consolation; he considers it unnatural that the boy should not overcome his grief for his mother by "thinking of others," as Sheppard does in his role as boys' counselor. Norton, greedy and dull, responds to Rufus Johnson partly because he fears the older boy and partly because Rufus's religious fundamentalism offers him something his father cannot give him. Like Francis Tarwater in *The Violent Bear It Away*, Rufus clings to his integrity; he insists, for instance, that there are places spaceships cannot go, reminding the reader of young Tarwater's contempt for airplanes: "I wouldn't give you nothing for no airplane. A buzzard can fly." So much for man's vaunted technological achievements.

Ironically, while Sheppard seeks to win the mind of the delinquent through books and a telescope, Rufus wins Norton's mind with the Bible and the telescope: the instrument of science is subverted to what Rufus would regard as greater truth. When Norton launches his flight into space, he chooses Rufus's world—and Miss O'Connor's world of "religious realities." Sheppard offers his son a physical existence with no meaning beyond what can be measured; Rufus offers an immaterial existence and immeasurable bliss.

Sheppard, disgraced and forced to admit his failure with Rufus after it becomes clear that Rufus has not renounced his life of vandalism, suddenly realizes that he has done everything for the older boy, even to the neglect of his own son. His remorse is great, for of course he has need of remorse—a sentimental repudiation of one "good" in exchange for another "good." He thinks of Norton as "all light," as the source of his salvation, and rushes to embrace the boy he has so lately ignored in order to prove his good faith to Rufus. He plans to promise that he will never fail Norton again and will be both mother and father to the boy; these vows reveal he has learned nothing yet from Rufus. If he still has Norton, to whom he may play Alpha and Omega, end-all and be-all, he will remain deified in his own mind as the omnipotent father figure; his secularist doctrine will remain intact, and both father and son will be irremediably lost.

Fortunately, Sheppard arrives at the attic too late: Norton is dead and Sheppard is left with nothing but a sense of his own inadequacy and of the satanic power which encourages man's belief in his human strength in order to take advantage of his weakness. The results of Sheppard's playing Jesus have been both futile and fatal: the intelligent delinquent he wanted to save has denied and reviled him, and his son has lost his life in order to find it. Sheppard's explanations of Rufus's desperate awareness of evil have precipitated tragedy and have also left Sheppard smirched with the terrible hint of perversion, a lie Rufus has hurled in his teeth in the presence of the police and a reporter.

Rufus recognizes the difference between faith and belief; he knows that faith is sometimes without cause and contrary to available evidence, but Sheppard has no concept of faith. Miss O'Connor dramatizes this point through Sheppard's protecting Rufus from the police on one occasion and permitting the police to take him to jail on another. The first time, he is certain that the boy could not have committed the crime for which he is sought; the second time, he suspects the boy to be guilty and gives him up to the law to "teach him a lesson." A Negro is arrested for the second crime, and Sheppard must humble himself to Rufus for losing faith in him. However, Rufus is found to be guilty of both crimes and flaunts his guilt in Sheppard's face. When Sheppard insists that Rufus's guilt has not shaken his resolution to save the boy despite himself, Rufus responds "Save yourself. . . . Nobody can save me but Jesus." Sheppard's reply epitomizes his attitude: " 'You don't deceive me,' he said. 'I flushed that out of your head in the reformatory. I saved you from that, at least.' The muscles in Johnson's face stiffened. A look of such repulsion hardened on his face that Sheppard drew back. The boy's eyes were like distorting mirrors in which he saw himself made hideous and grotesque. 'I'll show you,' Johnson whispered."[3]

Eventually Johnson does show Sheppard, just as young Tarwater defies Rayber's determinism by drowning Bishop. Rufus begins his "seduction" of Norton immediately after his showdown with Sheppard; the two boys begin reading the Bible together and talking conspiratorily.

In an argument over the Bible reading, Rufus eats a page from the Bible to prove his faith to the outraged Sheppard: "I've eaten it like Ezekiel and it was honey to my mouth," he says. Then wonder transforms his face: "I've eaten it like Ezekiel and I don't want none of your food after it nor no more ever." Sheppard, pushed to his limit, says, "Go then. Go. Go," sending Rufus from his home as the boy had predicted he finally would. The "transformed" Rufus, much like young Tarwater in his denial of earthly food, goes from Sheppard's home to perform one final act of vandalism in which he actively tries to be captured. He is brought back to Sheppard and reviles him again, concluding with his terrible charge that Sheppard has made "immor'l suggestions" to him. The context in which Rufus places the suggestions reveals Miss O'Connor's meaning in this story, which is almost exactly the meaning of *The Violent Bear It Away*. The reporter asks Rufus why he wanted to get caught: "The question and the sight of Sheppard seemed to throw the boy into a fury. 'To show up that big tin Jesus!' he hissed and kicked his leg out at Sheppard. 'He thinks he's God. I'd rather be in the reformatory than in his house, I'd rather be in the pen! The Devil has him in his power. He don't know his left hand from his right, he don't have as much sense as his crazy kid!' He paused and then swept on to his fantastic conclusion. 'He made suggestions to me!' " (p. 187). Pressed about the nature of the suggestions, Rufus says they were "immor'l" and adds, "But I ain't having none of it, I'm a Christian." Further pressed for details, Rufus says that Sheppard is a "dirty atheist" who has said "there wasn't no hell."

Rufus's idea of "immor'l suggestions" would clearly not stand up in court, but his meaning is fundamental to the story: seduction away from God, invitation to trust one's own power with no consideration of God's judgment, amounts to the ultimate immoral suggestion. Rufus realizes that morality is not merely a matter of doing good, or of not doing evil; it is a state of mind and a state of grace which cannot be achieved by the do-gooder whose deeds glorify himself. The secularist's good, though it may help the physical man, is potentially destructive of the spiritual man.

Sheppard's realization of Norton's death comes almost immediately after Rufus has been dragged away shrieking: "I lie and steal because I'm good at it! My foot don't have a thing to do with it! The lame shall enter first! The halt'll be gathered together. When I get ready to be saved, Jesus'll save me" (pp. 188–89). Attempting to justify his failure with Rufus, Sheppard realizes he has "ignored his own child to feed his vision of himself. . . . A rush of agonizing love for the child rushed over him like a transfusion of life. The little boy's face appeared to him transformed: the image of his salvation; all light" (p. 190). If any doubt of Sheppard's immorality remains, he stands convicted in these few lines; his love for the child is totally selfish: he would use the boy to "transfuse" life into himself. Like Rayber, who "uses" Bishop and thinks he cannot live without the idiot, Sheppard battens on the life and the soul of his son. The homosexual who emerged from the woods "as if he had refreshed himself on blood" could hardly be more reprehensible than Sheppard—that is, if one believes in "religious realities," as Miss O'Connor certainly did.

In *The Violent Bear It Away* Francis Tarwater's "friend" attempts to convince him that there is no Devil, just as Sheppard tries to convince Rufus. That friend, who later turns out to be the Devil, or Francis's "adversary," is associated with the homosexual who rapes Francis, leading to his rebirth. One of the friend's first acts, linking him with sexual perversion from the start, is to encourage Francis to get drunk: when he first tasted the liquor, which his uncle had forbidden him to drink, "a burning arm slid down Tarwater's throat as if the Devil were already reaching inside him to finger his soul." "It ain't Jesus or the Devil," says the friend. "It's Jesus or you." Sheppard preaches the same doctrine; he assumes that Rufus's intelligence demands that he deny the existence of the Devil and lead his life according to normal, material standards.

One may justify Sheppard's neglect of his own son on the basis of Rufus's greater need for help, but to do so overlooks the fact that

Sheppard's use of the delinquent boy is immoral in itself: Sheppard wants to project himself into Rufus's accomplishments because Norton disappoints him intellectually and "spiritually." (Norton is not generous and seems destined to "operate a small-loan company," p. 143.) The suggestion that Norton destroys himself because he has been neglected blurs the issue further; not physical or emotional neglect but spiritual neglect, depriving him of religious reality, leads to the child's suicide.

Rayber in the novel and Sheppard in the story are equally determined to secularize the boys with whom they must deal and from whom they expect self-gratification beyond what they may acquire from their own children. Both men live alone, one because his wife has left him and the other because his wife is dead, and both have dull-witted sons, though one is more deficient than the other. In both works the do-gooder (the adult determined to understand and save the incipient fanatic) ignores his own rush of revulsion toward the object of his efforts; and in both works the insistence of materialist, secular solutions to essentially religious problems drives the youngster to his act of violence. The same fascination apparently exists between Rufus and Norton as between Francis and Bishop, and in both works a gift symbolizing the materialism of contemporary life plays an important part in the resolution of conflicts. In this respect the short story is superior to the novel, for the telescope, suggestive of Sheppard's ambitions for both boys, provides the means for Rufus to give Norton a "slender channel to the stars," totally subverting Sheppard's scientism. The corkscrew in the novel, on the other hand, though one recognizes it as a perfect gift for Rayber to select, has no bearing on Francis's drowning Bishop, except insofar as the gift is Rayber's means of paving the way for his final discussion with Francis. (The gift, of course, is unnecessary, but Rayber assumes throughout the book that he can buy something for Francis to solidify their relationship.)

At the sight of his hanged son Sheppard "reeled back like a man on the edge of a pit." Rayber, in the novel, hears his son's bellows and realizes at once what has happened. He realizes that tomorrow "they would drag the pond for Bishop." So ends the story of Rayber; he does not appear again, but there is no doubt about what has happened to him or about how he completes the meaning of the novel.

Throughout the book appear hints of Bishop's importance to his father. The boy generates a feeling of "horrifying love" in Rayber, a useless, futureless love capable of throwing him "to the ground in an act of idiot praise." Rayber associates that love and its accompanying pain with the madness of fanaticism; to enforce this connection, Miss O'Connor reveals that Francis is shocked that Bishop looks like the dead prophet Mason Tarwater. However, without Bishop, Rayber's horrifying love would "avalanche" over everything "that his reason hated." In chapter six Bishop crawls into Rayber's lap and the "hated love" seizes him: "He knew that if he could once conquer this pain, face it and with a supreme effort of his will refuse to feel it, he would be a free man. He held Bishop rigidly. Although the child started the pain, he also limited it, contained it" (p. 388). At the end of the book Rayber "stood waiting for the raging pain, the intolerable hurt that was his due, to begin, so that he could ignore it, but he continued to feel nothing. He stood light-headed at the window and it was not until he realized there would be no pain that he collapsed" (p. 423). Like so many other O'Connor characters, Rayber believes that by denying his pain, his weakness, he will achieve what he considers "freedom." (Hulga in "Good Country People," for instance, uses her handicap as an instrument of denial.) Rayber says to Francis, "The other way is not so simple. It's the way I've chosen for myself. It's the way you take as a result of being born again the natural way— through your own efforts, your intelligence" (p. 418). Thus he believes that his effort to drown his idiot son conformed to what he regards as "rational" behavior. He recalls a newspaper photograph of someone giving Bishop artificial respiration, with Rayber "on his knees, watching with an agonized expression."

Rayber has been set free at the end of the novel's second section, not in the way he had expected—through his own efforts, his intelligence—but rather through what appears to be a senselessly violent act. The photograph of Rayber kneeling with an "agonized expression" before his son makes clear what he later loses with Bishop's death. That loss, leading to Rayber's rebirth, begins even before Bishop is dead; Rayber hears his son's bellows, and his hearing aid "made the sound seem to come from inside him as if something in him were tearing itself free." The hearing aid is another secular instrument which assumes metaphoric meaning in the novel: Rayber wears it as a result of old Tarwater's shotgun blast; it makes him look to Francis as if his head is wired, and the boy asks if he thinks with his head or with the "machine." It represents his deafness to God's word; it is also emblematic of King Jeroboam's withered hand in 1 Kings 13.

Had Miss O'Connor added a line to "The Lame Shall Enter First," which, fortunately, she did not, it would doubtless have been: "Sheppard stood light-headed in the attic and it was not until he realized there would be no pain that he collapsed." Both Rayber and Sheppard need their sons as objects to contain their love; both need dependents whom they can promise never to fail again and for whom they may assume Godlike roles. Neither can be saved from intellectual pride and overweening self-confidence as long as they have children from whom they can "transfuse" life.

Clearly, Tarwater's first step toward the realization of his mission is his drowning of Bishop; its effect on Rayber underlines the cyclical and reciprocal structure of the book, for Rayber has driven the boy to his deed. Similarly, Rufus is "transformed" after he eats the page from the Bible in defiance of Sheppard; though he had come to Sheppard in need and hunger, he leaves determined that he will never eat Sheppard's food again. He rejects "tin Jesus" charity as he rejects the idea of secular salvation: "Nobody can save me but Jesus." Rufus's seduction of Norton and Norton's suicide leave Sheppard no vestige of his old assurance: he has seen his "hideous and grotesque" image in Rufus's eyes, and that is the image with which he must now live. The death of Bishop fulfills the frequently reiterated phophecy in *The Violent Bear It Away*; the girl evangelist in chapter five speaks it, recognizing the nature of Rayber's pity and his spiritual deafness: "The Word of God is a burning Word to burn you clean, burns man and child, man and child the same, you people!" (p. 385). Both Rayber and Francis leave the tabernacle in a state of shock, which, as Rayber realizes later, brings them to a closeness out of which friendship could have been born had he taken advantage of the moment.

That night Rayber had "a wild dream in which he chased Tarwater through an interminable alley that twisted suddenly back on itself and reversed the roles of pursuer and pursued. The boy had overtaken him, given him a thunderous blow on the head, and then disappeared." Mason Tarwater had prophesied that Francis would burn Rayber's eyes clean; Rayber's dream reasserts the book's total structure as it foreshadows the grace which will descend upon him. In the dream Tarwater's "disappearance" is followed by an "over-whelming sense of release." Tarwater's flight into the darkness at the end of part two results in Rayber's final release from humanist idolatry, his realization that he has no pain to overcome after Bishop's death. The child evangelist, whom Rayber saw as "exploited," had said it all: the world seeks God's green seasons, the spring and summer of His will when, in fact, "love cuts like the cold wind and the will of God is plain as the winter" (p. 383).

Both "The Lame Shall Enter First" and *The Violent Bear It Away* focus on what Rayber would consider "unnatural" or involuntary rebirth, for in both works a death provides the necessary illumination. Sheppard's egocentric, tin-Jesus vow never again to fail his son is thwarted by the boy's self-destruction in quest of the spiritual goal about which Rufus has taught him. Similarly, Bishop's baptismal drowning begins the process of rebirth for both Rayber and Francis. For Francis the final vision is of another sacrament, the Holy Eucharist; obeying his last commandment, he accepts the sacrament of ordination. The short story also contains allusion to the Eucharist, underlined by Rufus Johnson's exclamation after eating a page from the Bible. He repudiates Sheppard's food after he tastes the honey of revelation. Likewise, though he is not sure why, Francis is unable to eat while he lives with his uncle, and when he does eat he is made ill. In his final revelation he understands that his hunger cannot be satisfied by earthly food; once he realizes this truth, he is again able to eat. A glance back at *Wise Blood* reveals further sacramental elements in Miss O'Connor's work: Haze Motes kills the false prophet Solace Layfield but leans over him to hear his confession; the destruction of the murder car by a "kindly" patrolman completes Haze's "conversion," his renunciation of the world and the beginning of his limited ministry.

Finally, the violated Tarwater, left naked in the woods, his hands tied with the lavender handkerchief "which his friend had thought of as an exchange" for his hat, is the reborn Tarwater. What more fitting reminder of man's helplessness in the grip of sin and what greater promise of sacramental redemption than the lavender color of penance? Purple is the liturgical color of Advent and Lent, seasons of preparation and penitence preceding the joyous festivals of Christmas and Easter.

In light of what one knows of Tarwater's "friend," actually the Devil, Tarwater's hands being tied suggests two nineteenth-century analogues. In *Billy Budd,* a work largely concerned with the relationship of innocence to evil, Melville observes that Billy's stutter is a reminder that the Devil has his hand in even the most perfect of human creations. Even more important is Hawthorne's "The Birthmark," in which Alymer seeks to remove a blemish from the otherwise flawless skin of his wife. That the birthmark is in the shape of a human hand is significant because of the association of hands with work (as in our frequent use of the word "hands" to designate "workmen"). One of the terms of the fall was that Adam and Eve had to earn their bread by the sweat of the brow.

At the end of *The Violent Bear It Away* the terrible speed of God's mercy expresses the same paradox as the child evangelist's earlier claim that "love cuts like the cold wind." Tarwater's rebirth drives him from the primal but explosive garden (Powderhead), but he goes forth with greater knowledge than did Adam, for whom redemption was but a plan and a promise. Francis Tarwater carries with him the mark of man's nature, but in that nature is his hope.

CHAPTER SIX

The Posthumous Collection

From the Garden of Eden to Judgment Day

HAVING ESTABLISHED the nature of Miss O'Connor's frame for *Everything That Rises Must Converge*, we must yet remark her thematic development in the remaining stories through the accumulation of significant symbols. Spectacles, for instance, recur in this collection as one of Miss O'Connor's means of establishing the difference between spiritual vision and physical sight. The Negro actor's hornrimmed glasses oppose the empty frames of Tanner's carved spectacles; the hornrims are a costume detail, but the carved spectacles lead to a revelation of common humanity. In the title story Miss O'Connor emphasizes the unmoored eye of Julian's dying mother; she had used almost precisely the same image in dramatizing Mrs. Shortley's death in "The Displaced Person." The collection also relies heavily on the recurrent image of the revelatory dark line of trees and on the passage past the dragon. As the ultimate convergence, the cessation of time in its ordinary sense, death marks the successful passing of the dragon.

In each story a self-sufficient character meets his "comeuppance," but in each story the action is presented in such a way as to permit hope of redemption or of a redemptive and "purifying terror." The doctrinal progression in the nine stories of *Everything That Rises Must Converge* is perhaps more pronounced than in *A Good Man Is Hard to Find,* for the white woman who dies in the title story experiences a regression at the time of her death, while at the end old Tanner has a vision of his resurrection. In both instances the end result for the chief characters is death, or, as Teilhard might say, diminishment. Tanner makes considerably more of his death than does the nameless woman of the title story, but this does not lessen the anagogical significance of her death.

"Everything That Rises Must Converge" first appeared in *New World Writing* in 1961. "Judgement Day," a revision of "The Geranium" (*Accent*, 1946), is one of Miss O'Connor's earliest stories. Its revisions further support the idea of her thematic consistency.

In the title story Julian, a young, unmarried man living with his mother, joyfully witnesses her humiliation on a bus as he accompanies her to her reducing lesson at the "Y." The unsuccessful son, spiritual kin to the protagonists in "The Partridge Festival" and "The Enduring Chill," longs vaguely to be a writer; he thinks that he has accepted the new social order of legislated equality and attempts to fraternize with the well-dressed Negroes on the bus. (He is snobbish and was horrified on one occasion to discover that a Negro whose friendship he had cultivated was a bookie.) Julian's annoyance with his mother is based on her ignorance of her own situation: she claims that she "knows who she is," but her sense of identity is apparently dependent upon a "good family" and former affluence. She has shared with Julian her memories of the old family home, and he longs desperately for the graceful life it represents.

Part of the humor of "Everything That Rises Must Converge" occurs with the mother's realization that a Negro woman who boards the bus is wearing a hat exactly like hers. Earlier in the story she had confided to Julian that her own hat was too expensive; she had paid a high price so she would not meet herself on the street. Miss O'Connor emphasizes the sameness of the two women by repeating exactly the description of their hats: "A purple velvet flap came down on one side of it and stood up on the other; the rest of it was green and looked like a cushion with the stuffing out."

Another repetition emphasizes Julian's similarity to a Negro man on the bus. Julian hid behind a newspaper to establish a "mental bubble . . . when he could not bear to be a part of what was going on around him." When the Negro boards the bus, he also hides behind his paper and ignores Julian's efforts to be friendly. Julian's mother immediately responds to the Negro child who sits near her, for she thinks that all children are cute but that Negro children are generally cuter than white ones. The child's mother sits next to Julian, and he realizes that the two women have, in a sense, exchanged sons, but he also realizes that his mother will not see the symbolic meaning of the scene.

The mother's sense of humor permits her to accept the humiliation of confronting a Negro wearing "her" hat, but she cannot understand that it is no longer appropriate for white women to give bits of change to Negro children. Julian wishes to prevent his mother's giving money to the child, but she is convinced that she must give the money; unable to find a nickel, she produces a shining, new penny. The Negress refuses to let her child take the money and angrily strikes the white woman to the sidewalk. Julian's response to the attack is that his mother deserved what she got; he hopes that she has learned her lesson. The event emphasizes his conviction that the world has changed and implies that his mother cannot retain her old identity in that changed world.

The mother rises from the sidewalk with dignity and insists upon returning home. Julian wants to take the bus, but she begins to walk; shortly she reveals that she has reverted to childhood and wishes to be taken care of like a child. Immediately after this regression she dies from a stroke which sends Julian running toward "a cluster of lights he saw in the distance ahead of him." But "the lights drifted farther away the faster he ran and his feet moved numbly as if they carried him nowhere. The tide of darkness seemed to sweep him back to her, postponing from moment to moment his entry into the world of guilt and sorrow" (p. 23).

Clearly, Julian is but "postponing . . . his entry into the world of guilt and sorrow," for that entry is bound to occur now that his mother is dead and he must admit his dependence on her and his callous treatment of her in her last minutes of life. The mother's loss of illusion, the shattering of the world in which she knew who she was, is more than she can bear, but mercifully her mind breaks and she returns to the security of the "old days" when she was a pampered child, cared for and loved. Julian has no such comfort. Ill-suited though he is for the decisions of the latter half of the twentieth century, he must learn to acknowledge reality, for he can no longer feed his self-esteem by shocking his mother with "liberal" actions. Like so many of Miss O'Connor's characters, Julian is brought face to face with his weaknesses and the moment of truth can offer nothing but hope. "Judgement Day" bears the same relationship to

"Everything That Rises Must Converge" that "The Displaced Person" bears to "A Good Man Is Hard to Find." In both collections Miss O'Connor apparently amplified shorter, previously published stories for the express purpose of completing a fictional frame and achieving her doctrinal progression. This belief is supported by her novelistic method: revision of stories to function in continuous narrative frames.

In the original story, "The Geranium," out of which "Judgement Day" grew, an old southerner living in New York tastes humility in an encounter with a sophisticated and mildly patronizing Negro, after which he is insulted by a neighbor whose potted geranium he has looked forward to seeing every day. The original story clearly lacks unity; the geranium episode merely follows in time the other event. The revised story generates significant metaphysical meaning from the same basic situation but omits the geranium in favor of developing the character of the transplanted Georgian. Both stories juxtapose old Tanner's reactions to the New York Negro with his intimate friendship with a "nigger" back home, but the revised version is far richer, far more suggestive, in its ironic use of these materials.

In the title story of the final collection Julian's response to his mother's death reveals his vulnerability and dependence; he is poorly prepared for dealing with "guilt and sorrow" on his own. In the concluding story old Tanner's death apparently has a similar effect on his "duty-doing" daughter; she reneges on her promise to have his body returned to Georgia for burial, "but after she had done it she could not sleep at night." The last paragraph ends, "so she had him dug up and shipped the body to Corinth. Now she rests well at night and her good looks have mostly returned."

Neither Julian nor Tanner's daughter is concerned with spiritual matters; both are concerned with "practical" matters and with appearances. The central revelations occur to members of the older generation. Julian's mother fully experiences the extent of her displacement; her stroke is very similar to the violent wrenching of personal identity which Mrs. Shortley experiences in "The Displaced Person." As Julian's mother was dying, "her face was fiercely distorted. One eye, large and staring, moved slightly to the left as if it had become unmoored. The other remained fixed on him, raked his face again, found nothing and closed" (p. 23). As Mrs. Shortley was dying, "all at once her fierce expression faded into a look of astonishment and her grip on what she had loosened. One of her eyes drew near to the other and seemed to collapse quietly and she was still."

Similarly, at the climaxes of their experiences both Tanner and Julian's mother experience fantasy reunions with loved ones. "Tell Caroline to come get me," the sick woman says, obviously alluding to a Negro servant in better days. Tanner assumes that his Negro friend Coleman will meet the train on which he fancies his body is traveling homeward for burial, and at the high point of his dream he imagines himself greeting Coleman with the news of the resurrection of the body on judgment day.

Tanner attains a spiritual victory while externally suffering humiliation and defeat. Living in New York with his daughter, he regrets his decision to leave Georgia rather than to operate his still for the mixed-blooded Dr. Foley, who had bought the property on which Tanner and Coleman lived. In a sense Tanner has been displaced by a part-Negro, part-Indian, part-white man whom he resents in a way similar to the Shortleys's resentment of Guizac. The racial issue is brought to the foreground by Foley's observing that the day is coming when "the white folks IS going to be working for the colored and you mights well to git ahead of the crowd." Tanner is true to type with his rejoinder that "the government ain't got around yet to forcing the white folks to work for the colored."

Tanner, then, with his racial pride, is the author of his own misery in New York; he finally admits to himself that he would have preferred being "a nigger's white nigger any day" to "sitting here looking out of this window all day in this no-place." At the beginning of his relationship with Coleman, Tanner had put the Negro in his place; now, ironically, as he awaits death, he wants Coleman to put him in his place—bury him in Georgia clay. Though he is shocked that a Negro should live next door to his daughter, he had lived for years with Coleman in their jerry-built shack. Anxious to know the Negro next door, whom he assumes to be like Georgia Negroes he has known, Tanner treats the actor as he would other Negroes, sawmill workers and domestics, but he is fascinated by the actor's hornrimmed glasses and by the Negro woman's bronze hair. The Negro rebuffs him from the start; he objects to being called "preacher" and denies being from the South. In particular, he repudiates all religion, declaring that he does not believe any of "that crap." Old Tanner replies, "And you ain't black . . . and I ain't white."

At the end of "Judgement Day" Tanner attempts to run away to catch a freight for Georgia but falls sick on the stairs, where his coffin-dream and his reunion with Coleman are interrupted by the Negro actor. Just as he imagines that he is leaping from his casket to shout "Judgement Day!" to Coleman, he mutters Coleman's name, and the actor, offended already at being called "preacher," assumes that Tanner is calling him a "coal man." He denies being a "coal man" and says "in a mocking voice," " 'Judgement day. Ain't no judgement day, old man. Cept this. Maybe this here judgement day for you' " (p. 268). There follows the outrage of Tanner's head being forced between the banister rails, but Miss O'Connor does not dramatize that violence, just as she does not dramatize the rape of Francis Tarwater. Tanner's last words, "Hep me up, Preacher, I'm on my way home," make no impression on the appearance-conscious Negro actor, but they are an economical summary of Miss O'Connor's total fictional theme: movement upward and movement homeward, even when the homebound character must first be totally displaced from physical things in order to recognize the nature of his "true country." Haze Motes's dying words, "I want to go on where I'm going," are followed by Mrs. Flood's triumphant words, "I see you've come home!"

Miss O'Connor's biblical emphases in "Judgement Day" are an interesting combination of the Petrine and the Pauline. Tanner's home is in Corinth, Georgia. Peter is said to have established the church at Corinth, and Paul's first epistle to the Corinthians contains the convert's eloquent testimony of belief in the resurrection of Christ as a benefit conferred on all believers (1 Cor. 15). Peter is known as the Apostle to the Gentiles because of his conversion of Cornelius (Acts 10), and he was at the house of "one Simon a tanner" when he was summoned to testify to Cornelius; hence Miss O'Connor links the Petrine with Tanner and with the Christian's rising above national and racial differences to converge in faith with all other Christians. (Allusion to Romans 9 and to *The Waste Land*, part four, makes the same point implicit in *Wise Blood*.) Tanner's initial attitude toward the Negro Coleman is comparable to Saul's early persecution of the Christians, and his thrice-repeated refusal of Dr. Foley's offer of employment parallels Peter's denial of Christ. Coleman was paroled to Tanner and remained with him for thirty years, the number of years of Christ's preparation for his three-year ministry. Finally, Tanner's death—his hat pulled down over his face and his head and arms thrust through the banister rails—is suggestive of both martyrs' deaths: Paul was beheaded and Peter was crucified upside down. Miss O'Connor specifies that Tanner landed upside down when he fell on the stairs and that when his daughter later found him, his "feet dangled over the stairwell like a man in the stocks."

Early in his relationship with Coleman, Tanner had feared the Negro and had intended to threaten him with a knife he carried constantly while supervising his work gang. (He whittled nervously, dropping carved figures in the dust and immediately beginning others.) For some reason, however, instead of threatening Coleman ("Nigger, this knife is in my hands now, but it will be in your gut shortly"), he finds himself carving a pair of spectacles which he gives to the Negro. The spectacles bind the two men together, and Coleman becomes "a negative image" of Tanner; their convergence is their recognition of their common lot of "clownishness and captivity" (p. 255). Such a convergence is impossible with the Negro actor, who judges people wholly on externals and wears his hornrimmed glasses as a costume detail. Like the "Parrum nigger" in *Wise Blood* whose "sour triumphant voice" proclaims that "Jesus been a long time gone," he denies faith and human need out of pride.

Inappropriate Convergences in "The Partridge Festival"

Everything That Rises Must Converge contains nine stories, one of which, "Parker's Back," replaces an earlier story, "The Partridge Festival," originally intended for the collection.[1] One may wonder why "Parker's Back" could not have been added without omitting "The Partridge Festival." There are two possible reasons: either "The Partridge Festival" is an inferior story, or it is inappropriate for the collection. We shall see that the latter is true.

In the first collection "The Displaced Person" provides the "good man," the one among many, or, as it is expressed in Job (one of the biblical sources for "Parker's Back") one among a thousand: "If there be a messenger with him, an interpreter, one among a thousand, to show unto man his uprightness: Then he is gracious unto him, and saith, Deliver him from going down to the pit: I have found a ransom" (Job 33:23–24). This Old Testament prophecy of the vicarious atonement applies perfectly to "The Displaced Person," and it underlines the function of that story as part of *A Good Man's* fictional frame; it is equally relevant to *Everything That Rises*, in which each of the stories assumes the fact of original sin but also affirms the fact of redemption. The frame of the latter collection illustrates the doctrinal progression: entry into the world of guilt and sorrow begins the book, but old Tanner's good death at the end testifies that this is a redeemed world for the faithful.

Rebirth is a part of redemption, and spiritual rebirth depends upon man's ability to change, specifically, to transcend the physical facts of life according to the promptings of inner vision (or, in Teilhard's terms, to expand one's consciousness). Clearly, several stories in the second collection carry Miss O'Connor's concern with redemption further than she had ever gone before: in "The Enduring Chill," for instance, she daringly seeks to realize the descent of the Holy Ghost upon a chastened and receptive Asbury Fox. "Parker's Back" dramatizes one man's discovery of his Christian identity through experiences parallel to those of Old Testament prophets. Obviously there was no place in the collection for a story which concludes with the central character's realization of his heredity (carnal and "commercial" instincts) which "stopped [him] . . . and *fixed him where he was*" (italics ours). Miss O'Connor's withdrawn story, "The Partridge Festival," is such a work: it dramatizes the futility of the humanist quest for perfect heroes; that futility is brought to its climax by the central character's self-realization, which "seemed to have been waiting there from all time to claim him." Hope of redemption in such a story is neither expressed nor implied: this is a story of convergence but not a story of transcendence.

"The Partridge Festival" is about a would-be artist's quest for values. Calhoun, grandson of the man who inaugurated the annual azalea festival in the town of Partridge and who coined the town's motto—"Beauty is our money crop"—attends the festival to gather material for a book. He has read the newspaper account of the murder of six citizens by a community crackpot, Singleton; among the newspaper photographs of the murderer and his victims Calhoun has found Singleton's "the only distinctive face in the lot." He regards the victims as "of the same general stamp as his great-grandfather," whose miniature portrait Calhoun's aunts show him every time he visits. He regards Singleton as a victim of the "madness around him," for Singleton's act of violence followed his imprisonment in the stocks and then in a privy after a mock trial for the "crime" of refusing to buy an "Azalea Badge" in support of the annual festival. All these opinions Calhoun bases on surface impressions; he knows nothing about Singleton, though he hopes to write a book which will exonerate the murderer and condemn the community for its crass values and its prostitution of azaleas: "He expected to write something that would vindicate the madman and he expected the writing of it to mitigate his own guilt, for his doubleness, his shadow, was cast before him more darkly than usual in the light of Singleton's purity." (Calhoun's "doubleness" refers to his working as a salesman in the summer, making enough money by selling boats and air conditioners to support himself as artist and bohemian during the winter.) Singleton's likeness in the newspaper burns in Calhoun's imagination "like a dark reproachful liberating star." He sees Singleton as a Christ figure, and he sets out determinedly to find citizens who will corroborate his belief that Singleton represents a cause—freedom, or individualism—and that Singleton's violence was in expiation for the sins of the community, which only he transcended.

Calhoun is convinced that Singleton's imprisonment, first in the privy and then in the state mental hospital, qualifies him as a "Sacrificial lamb." An afternoon's efforts reveal no evidence to support this evaluation of Singleton; frustrated, Calhoun returns to his aunts' home and discovers that the old ladies have arranged a date for him to attend the beauty pageant that night with Mary Elizabeth, the girl next door, whom Calhoun infers to be retarded because of her round, childish face. To their mutual horror, Mary Elizabeth and Calhoun discover they have a great deal in common: each regards Singleton as a Christ figure and each intends to write about him— she in a factual exposé and he in a novel. They goad one another into visiting the hospital to see Singleton. It is necessary for the couple to claim to be relatives of the madman, and they tell the necessary lie: seeing the visiting permits bearing their assumed names, "both appeared to recognize that in their common kinship with him a kinship with each other was unavoidable." Earlier, Calhoun had anticipated his visit to Singleton as a "torturing experience" which "might be his salvation," for it might "raise him once and for all from his commercial instincts." On the hospital grounds he has a brief vision of Singleton and is certain that meeting his "Saviour" will "effect a change in him, that after this visit, some strange tranquility he had not before conceived of would be his."

Calhoun and Mary Elizabeth see Singleton only briefly, for the madman enters cursing in a machinelike way and rapidly reveals illusions of material grandeur and sexual attractiveness. He thinks he owns the "hotel" in which he is staying, and he boasts that he is "well-fixed" and that there is "nobody in Partridge" he can't "skin." He makes suggestive noises to Mary Elizabeth, breaks free of his guards, and leaps atop a table where he throws his hospital gown over his head. The two devotees, who had felt "already joined in a predestined convergence" as they awaited Singleton, flee the hospital; after going five miles, Calhoun stops the car: "They sat silently, looking at nothing until finally they turned and looked at each other. There each saw at once the likeness of their kinsman and flinched. They looked away and then back, as if with concentration, they might find a more tolerable image." The joint humanist quest concludes not with the discovery of common kinship to the savior they sought, but a realization that they share the very qualities each had sought to repudiate and to condemn in the citizens of Partridge. Calhoun, leaning toward Mary Elizabeth in despair, is "stopped by a miniature visage which rose incorrigibly in her spectacles and fixed him where he was." The miniature visage is his reflection in her glasses, identical to the portrait of his great-grandfather he has lately seen at his aunts' home. "Round, innocent, undistinguished as an iron link, it was the face whose gift of life had pushed straight forward to the future to raise festival after festival. Like a master salesman, it seemed to have been waiting there from all time to claim him" (p. 85).

Miss O'Connor's implications are apparent: Calhoun is obliged to recognize his kinship with the spirit of Partridge, a compound of lechery and greed. He had refused to admit his resemblance to his great-grandfather's portrait, declaring himself a "different type entirely." But the shattering of his delusions about Singleton makes him recognize his kinship with the "gift of life" which had "raised festival after festival," each dedicated to materialistic ends and each subverting the natural procreative beauty of those ends. Though Calhoun has come to recognize his kinship with Mary Elizabeth, with Singleton, and with the spirit of Partridge, that realization occasions no hope: he was stopped where he was by the facts of heredity and of human nature which "seemed to have been waiting there from all time to claim him. His humanistic glorification of the spirit of man fails to save him from his "commercial instinct," and the story unequivocally ties him to the common lot of man—the terms of existence inherited by all men after the fall.

"The Partridge Festival" by its very title suggests the Devil's role and the necessity of the carnal in man's life. Folk culture frequently associates the partridge with lasciviousness. George Ferguson lists three different implications for the partridge: the good, or honorific, significance is truth, or the Church; the more general associations are with theft and deceit and with the Devil.[2] Ferguson cites Jeremiah 17:11: "As the partridge sitteth on eggs, and hatcheth them not; so he that getteth riches, and not by right, shall leave them in the midst of his days, and at his end shall be a fool." As is often the case, Miss O'Connor seems to have drawn her theme and images from her scriptural source, for Jeremiah 17 opens with the statement that "the sin of Judah is written with a pen of iron," an image echoed in the final description of Calhoun's face as "round, innocent, undistinguished as an iron link." The fifth verse is an explicit statement of Miss O'Connor's theme: "Thus saith the Lord: Cursed be the man that trusteth in man, and maketh flesh his arm, and whose heart departeth from the Lord."

As with most effective literary symbolism, "The Partridge Festival" contains internal evidence which makes knowledge of the bird's biblical and cultural associations unnecessary. The town's motto and the young people's accusation that the town prostitutes azaleas make the associations explicit. Singleton's imprisonment in the privy with a goat introduces another symbol of carnality; thus it is no surprise to learn that besides being grasping and stingy he is also lecherous: he epitomizes the spirit of Partridge rather than transcending it as the two young people had hoped. Their secular quest brings them back to the hard facts of man's need for redemption by a power outside himself. But no such redemption occurs in the story.

"Parker's Back," on the other hand, is a story of redemption and of rebirth expressed through O. E. Parker's assuming a prophetic role; he becomes Obadiah Elihue as a result of two "miracles" drawn directly from the Old Testament sources of his name. Both stories demonstrate Miss O'Connor's reliance upon, and fidelity to, scriptural sources, but they are thematically quite different.

Parker, a fruit and vegetable peddler, finds himself joylessly married to a plain and repressive religious fanatic. She objects to the idolatry of churches and to the tattoos which cover the front of Parker's body. To please his wife, he resists the desire for a final tattoo; he recognizes that he would not be able to enjoy a picture on his back and regrets that because his wife does not appreciate art she would not enjoy it either. But after a near escape from death in a tractor accident which ignites a tree and his shoes, which have been wrenched from his feet, he rushes to town to have a "picture of God" tattooed on his back. He selects a terrible, intense Byzantine head of Christ. He shows the tattoo to friends in the poolhall and attempts to throw them out when they laugh about it. When he returns home to show it to his wife, she denies that anyone knows what God looks like and condemns the picture as idolatrous. The conventional image of Jesus does not represent God for her. She drives him from their house and locks it; one last sees Parker outside, crying piteously beneath a tree.

Parker's unrealistic gesture marks him as a changed man; the tattoo which he cannot see and which his wife despises will be with him forever, disrupting his marriage and peace of mind. The great difference between this story and "The Partridge Festival" is precisely that Christ, not a realization of human sinfulness, has made the difference for Parker. Calhoun's recognition of his iron-linked tie with the past and with commercialism is unmitigated; his quest for a human savior led to disillusionment. He loses his humanist hope, but he does not gain a spiritual hope. For Parker, however, the tractor accident is a warning of mortality leading to positive action, not despair.

At first O. E. Parker is ashamed of his Christian name. During their courtship, when he had whispered "what them letters are the short of" to Sarah Ruth Cates, "her face slowly brightened as if the name came as a sign to her . . . 'Obadiah,' she said. The name still stank in Parker's estimation. 'Obadiah Elihue,' she said in a reverent voice. 'If you call me that aloud, I'll bust your head open,' Parker said" (p. 229). Returning home after the tattooing, eager to show his "picture of God" to his fundamentalist wife and certain she will recognize and understand it, Parker finds the door locked. Sarah refuses to open it when he identifies himself as O. E. "I don't know no O. E.," she says. Finally "Parker bent down and put his mouth near the stuffed keyhole. 'Obadiah,' he whispered and all at once he felt the light pouring through him turning his spider web soul into a perfect arabesque of colors, a garden of trees and birds and beasts. 'Obadiah Elihue!' he whispered. The door opened and he stumbled in" (p. 243).

Obadiah Elihue Parker's name is of great importance in "Parker's Back," for his use of the full name marks his rebirth, and the name provides an important source for the plot. (Similarly, in *The Violent Bear It Away* young Tarwater affirms his own name and rejects Rayber's name for him.) Only after Parker was reborn as the man with Christ on his back, fulfilling an Old Testament prophecy, did he feel "the light pouring through him." Parker's desire for tattoos had been insatiable; it had begun when he was fourteen and saw a circus performer "flexing his muscles so that the arabesque of men and beasts and flowers on his skin appeared to have subtle motion of its own." A new tattoo satisfied him for a month before he longed for another, but the tattoos were obviously not what he really sought: "The effect was not of one intricate arabesque of colors but of something haphazard and botched." His "enormous dissatisfaction" grew and the spaces "on the front of him for tattoos decreased," for he "had no desire for one anywhere he could not readily see it himself."

The intuitive and compulsive selection of the "picture of God" to be put on his back and the identification of himself as Obadiah Elihue indicate that he has accepted his role as prophet of the destruction of the Edomites, as recorded in the vision of Obadiah in the Old Testament. He has already shown his difference by fighting with his former cronies in the poolhall. As she frequently does, Miss O'Connor reinforces the biblical parallels here with numerous specific details, enriching the story for the Bible student or for those readers willing to accept her terms and pursue her hints. William A. Fahey believes that Parker's search for some greater value is represented in his torturing himself with tattoos, a torture Fahey describes as Parker's being "haunted by the absolute."[3] However, he does not deal with the biblical parallels in the story.

The book of Obadiah follows the book of Amos and contains a vision of the destruction of Edom, as prophesied in Amos 1:11. In the eighth chapter of Amos, the prophet is shown a basket of summer fruit and the Lord tells him: "The end is come upon my people of Israel; I will not again pass by them any more" (Amos 8:2). Later (verse 11) the Lord says: "Behold the days come that I will send a famine in the land, not a famine of bread, nor a thirst for water, but of hearing the words of the Lord." O. E.'s occupation and his apparent thirst for the word of God, despite his denials, allude to these passages in Amos. In the city he meets mockery on all sides—in the tattoo artist's studio and in the poolhall. The destruction of Edom is the destruction of the sons of Esau, son of Isaac and older brother of Jacob. Esau says to his brother, "Behold, I am at the point to die, and what profit shall this birthright do to me?" (Gen. 25:32). Recalling that the birthright is the father's blessing, and consequently God's blessing, one is justified in comparing Esau's question with Job's question, as stated by Elihu: "For thou saidst, What advantage will it be unto thee [God]? and, What profit shall I have if I be cleansed from my sin?" (Job 35:3).

Esau means "the red," and *Edom* comes from a primitive root meaning "to make or do." Esau the hunter is apparently more concerned with his physical than with his spiritual needs; consequently he relinquishes his birthright though he later wheedles a blessing of sorts from Isaac. According to the vision of Obadiah, Edom is destroyed for its "violence against thy brother Jacob," the chosen of *the Lord* (Obad. 1:10). Metaphorically, however, Esau's sin is secularism, or materialism—the elevation of the physical over the spiritual.

Apparently Parker is associated with Edom in the early parts of the story; his Christian name also associates him with the prophet who reports the vision. Verses three and four of the book of Obadiah, for instance, allude to the mountain which Edom occupies and to the Edomites' efforts to associate themselves with the eagle ("thou that dwellest in the clefts of the rock" and "though thou exalt thyself as the eagle"). In Miss O'Connor's story Sarah Ruth Cates declares that she likes none of O. E. Parker's tattoos but admits that "the chicken is not as bad as the rest." " 'What chicken?' Parker almost yelled. She pointed to the eagle" (p. 226).

At first Parker's attitude toward being saved, expressed to Sarah Ruth and to the tattoo artist, reveals that he considers salvation purely physical. He tells Sarah Ruth that "he didn't see it was anything in particular to save him from," and to the artist's mocking question, "Are you saved?" he says, "I ain't got no use for none of that. A man can't save his self from whatever it is don't deserve none of my sympathy." But his words "seemed . . . to evaporate at once as if he had never uttered them" (p. 238).

The first verse of the book of Obadiah reads: "We have heard a rumour from the Lord, and an ambassador is sent among the heathen, Arise ye, and let us rise up against her in battle." Obadiah Parker also hears a rumor from the Lord, as he testifies with his cry "GOD ABOVE!" when he crashes into the tree and sees his shoes eaten by the fire. He goes among the heathen, the blasphemers in the poolhall, and "rises up against them": "Parker lunged into the midst of them and like a whirlwind on a summer's day there began a fight that raged amid overturned tables and swinging fists until two of them grabbed him and ran to the door with him and threw him out. Then a calm descended on the pool hall as nerve shattering as if the long barn-like room were the ship from which Jonah had been cast into the sea" (pp. 240–41). As usual, Miss O'Connor has not permitted her biblical source to limit her choice of images, but her allusion to Jonah makes explicit the prophetic role which descends upon Parker because of the "rumour from the Lord." The Bible student will recall that Jonah follows Obadiah and that the great storm at sea results from Jonah's disobeying the Lord. The sailors cast Jonah into the sea "and the sea ceased from her raging. Then the men feared the Lord exceedingly, and offered a sacrifice unto the Lord, and made vows" (Jon. 1:15, 16). Although Parker, like Jonah, does not fully realize it, he has already begun his vocation.

Miss O'Connor's use of the word "whirlwind" in the poolhall scene is associated with still another biblical source, the scene in the book of Job in which Elihu remonstrated with Job for attempting to justify himself rather than admitting his deficiencies and accepting God's will. This allusion is closely related to the materials drawn from the book of Obadiah, once again illustrating Miss O'Connor's flexible use of biblical parallels.

The second and third verses of Obadiah further explicate the meaning of "Parker's Back": "Behold, I have made thee small among the heathen; thou art greatly despised. The pride of thine heart hath deceived thee, thou that dwellest in the clefts of the rock, whose habitation is high; that saith in his heart, Who shall bring me down to the ground." Parker's wife and his employer (the old woman he describes to Sarah Ruth as a "hefty blond") both heap scorn upon him; the tattoo artist at first refuses to serve him, thinking he is drunk, and later decides that he is crazy. Obviously the pride of Parker's heart has deceived him, for his desire to be like the small, sturdy man he had seen in the circus is not fulfilled until after he has been brought to the ground, crawling on his knees away from the flaming tree. ("He scrambled backwards, still sitting, his eyes cavernous, and if he had known how to cross himself he would have done it. . . . His truck was on a dirt road at the edge of the field. He moved toward it, still sitting, still backwards, but faster and faster; halfway to it he got up and began a kind of forward-bent run from which he collapsed on his knees twice.") Throughout the story Parker's pride is indicated by his wonder that he was ever attracted to his ugly, joyless wife and that, once married to her, he does not leave her when she becomes pregnant. The final link between Parker and the vision of Obadiah is established with the location of Parker's shack "on a high embankment overlooking a highway."

"Parker's Back" is another of Miss O'Connor's stories about a Christian *malgré lui*: Parker does not understand why he suddenly wants a picture of God on his back, and he continues to deny that he has been saved until after the poolhall fight; then, sitting on the ground behind the poolhall, he examines his soul. "He saw it as a spider web of facts and lies that was not at all important to him but which appeared to be necessary in spite of his opinion. The eyes that were now forever on his back were eyes to be obeyed. He was as certain of it as he had ever been of anything" (p. 241). Thinking of Sarah

Ruth, Parker gets to his feet: "She would know what he had to do. She would clear up the rest of it, and she would at least be pleased. It seemed to him that, all along, that was what he wanted, to please her." Like Tarwater, whose burnt eyes saw even familiar territory as "strange and alien country," Parker feels "as if he were himself a stranger to himself, driving into a new country though everything he saw was familiar to him, even at night." Mrs. Shortley, Mrs. May, and other characters in Miss O'Connor's works also find themselves in that new country.

The ironic conclusion of "Parker's Back" is that Sarah Ruth is not pleased. "God don't *look*," she tells Parker. "He's a spirit. No man shall see his face." In a significant twisting of truth she accuses him of "enflaming [himself] with idols under every green tree!" Finally "she grabbed up the broom and began to thrash him across the shoulders with it." "Parker was too stunned to resist. He sat there and let her beat him until she had nearly knocked him senseless and large welts had formed on the face of the tattooed Christ." Still gripping the broom, Sarah Ruth "looked toward the pecan tree and her eyes hardened still more. There he was—who called himself Obadiah Elihue—leaning against the tree, crying like a baby" (p. 244).

Sarah Ruth's denial of Parker's right to his prophetic name in no sense invalidates the experience which has led to his assumption of his prophetic role. Rather, her hardened eyes reveal that Parker's last secular and physical rationalization has been taken away. He had decided that "all along, that was what he wanted, to please her." Earlier he had decided not to look at the completed tattoo, "that all his sensations of the day and night before were those of a crazy man and that he would return to doing things according to his own sound judgement." Neither the claim that he chose the tattoo from madness nor the claim that he chose it to please Sarah Ruth could prevent the "all-demanding eyes" from inflicting their will upon him.

Parker's tattoo is permanent, and in a sense it supersedes Sarah Ruth: "Her sharp tongue and ice-pick eyes were the only comfort he could bring to mind," but even her eyes "appeared soft and dilatory compared with the eyes" of the suffering Christ. She screams at him that she can stand "lies and vanity" but that she doesn't want "no idolator in this house!" There seems little temporal hope for

Parker at the end of the story: his marital happiness, what little there was of it, has been destroyed by his tattoo, and he is left with "nothing on earth" to comfort him. But the central hope of "Parker's Back," the vision, recurs late in the story as a prelude to Parker's temporary rapture of discovering his "spider web soul," a perfect image for the spiritual transfiguration of his once external aspiration.

The vision at the center of the story results from Parker's carelessness in operating the tractor: man does not deserve grace; it merely comes. Time ceased to be relevant as Parker was prepared for the vision; he was thinking of a suitable design for his back when "the sun, the size of a golf ball, began to switch regularly from in front to behind him, but he appeared to see it both places as if he had eyes in the back of his head. All at once he saw the tree reaching out to grasp him" (p. 232). Parker's circling the field causes the sun "to switch," but the effect of the switching is visionary. In "an unbelievably loud voice: he yells "GOD ABOVE!" and sees his shoes "quickly being eaten by the fire." (This image may have been drawn from one of the many accounts of the movement of the sun at Fatima; the Bible contains no exact parallel to this miracle, but see 2 Kings 20.)

When Parker returns home after the tattooing, his wife asks, "Who's there?" and the vision recurs: "Parker turned his head as if he expected someone behind him to give him the answer. The sky had lightened slightly and there were two or three streaks of yellow floating above the horizon. Then as he stood there, a tree of light burst over the skyline. Parker fell back against the door as if he had been pinned there by a lance" (p. 242).

Parker identifies himself as Obadiah Elihue because his old identity is gone and his new one is almost complete. Although the significance of his name is largely derived from Elihu's role in the book of Job, the story is not so much concerned with providing exact biblical parallels as it is with dramatization of spiritual truth. However, Miss O'Connor has obviously drawn some details from Elihu's reproof of Job and his false friends (Job 32–37). For instance, Elihu makes clear that God need not justify His ways to man but that he sometimes comes to men in visions "that he may withdraw man from his purpose and hide pride from man" (Job 33:14–17). In Job 33 there are direct analogues to Parker's life and to the vicarious atonement. Married to Sarah Ruth, Parker loses weight, he is nervous and irritable, and fears for his sanity; then, almost as if Miss O'Connor were following the verses in order, there occur the accident with the tractor and what Parker takes to be his miraculous salvation.

> He is chastened also with pain upon his bed, and the multitude of his bones with strong pain;
> So that his life abhoreth bread, and his soul dainty meat;
> His flesh is consumed away, that it cannot be seen; and his bones that were not seen stick out.
> Yea, his soul draweth near unto the grave, and his life to the destroyers.
> If there be a messenger with him, an interpreter, one among a thousand, to show unto man his uprightness:
> Then he is gracious unto him, and saith, Deliver him from going down to the pit: I have found a ransom.
>
> (Job 33:19–24)

The ransom, of course, is Christ.

In the concluding sentence of the story Sarah Ruth sees the man "who called himself Obadiah Elihue—leaning against the tree, crying like a baby." This too is fulfillment of prophecy, necessary to Parker's achievement of his new self. The New Testament analogue is the well-known command beginning "Unless you be as a little child"; Elihu's statement is remarkably similar: "His flesh shall be fresher than a child's: he shall return to the days of his youth" (Job 33:25). Elihu continues, "Surely it is meet to be said unto God, I have borne chastisement, I will not offend any more" (Job 34:31). The chastized, weeping Parker is the reborn Obadiah Elihue.

Chapters 35 through 37 of Job, all spoken by Elihu, return frequently to cloud and light images, suggestive of the "streaks of yellow" Parker sees "floating above the horizon" just before "a tree of light burst over the skyline." Miss O'Connor frequently uses clouds to embody religious meanings. In "Revelation" Mrs. Turpin sees a purple streak in the sky which becomes a bridge bearing "a vast horde of souls . . . rumbling toward heaven." In *Wise Blood* a single cloud in the sky changes shape from the traditional image of God the Father to that of the Holy Ghost: "The blinding white cloud had turned into a bird with long thin wings and was disappearing in the opposite direction." O. E. Parker obeys Elihu's injunction: "Look into the heavens, and see; and behold the clouds which are higher than thou" (Job 35:5).

Because Miss O'Connor's story is an excellent one, Parker's experiences are characterized by what Teilhard called the "rigour and harmony of a natural process of evolution," and the reader does not feel cheated at the end when he realizes that Parker has been incorporated in Christ—or in God. Parker's ignorance and impatience with the distinctions among the persons of the Trinity make his total assimilation all the more real. As she does elsewhere, Miss O'Connor enforces Parker's choice with masterfully humorous profanity. The tattoo artist asks if Parker wants "Father, Son, or Spirit," and he answers, "Just God. Christ. I don't care. Just so it's God." No clearer statement of devout Trinitarianism could be devised. Far from comforting Parker, the physical imposition of the image of Christ onto his back sears the man's life; nothing can ever be the same for him again, and in the final beating, Christ suffers in him and he in Christ as the welts form on the tattooed face.

The substitution of "Parker's Back" for "The Partridge Festival" permits Miss O'Connor's posthumous collection to continue its thematic affirmation of the hope inherent in man's fall from grace. The fall stipulates the physical terms of man's existence, but God's redemptive plan enables him to transcend the physical. The collection, bound together with numerous convergences and revelations, proceeds from a young man's entry into the world of guilt and sorrow to an old man's vision of resurrection. Julian, in a real sense, is Adam, for his guilt and sorrow promise their own rewards; Tanner transcends Adam by his recognition of his brotherhood with Coleman.

To have broken the pattern of the collection with a story in which the "intolerable image" of kinship and the "miniature visage . . . rose incorrigibly . . . and fixed him where he was" would have been to abandon a doctrinal consistency which had informed Miss O'Connor's novels and her earlier collection of stories. From *Wise Blood* to *Everything That Rises Must Converge,* Flannery O'Connor insisted not so much on human depravity as upon the orthodox belief that salvation is for sinners and that God's plan for redemption depends upon a fall and upon judgment, whereas the secular society she castigated in all her works would deny that evil has a place in a world of advancing technology whose environmental controls make it possible for every man to be a "success." Perhaps she was compelled to repeat in "The Partridge Festival" that man's needs are in part physiological, dependent upon heredity and upon the result of the original fall from grace, but she wisely recognized that such a doctrinal utterance had no place in her last and most optimistic statement of belief.

Toward a Divine Center of Convergence

In an earlier chapter *The Violent Bear It Away* and "The Lame Shall Enter First" were considered together in order to establish the essential similarities of the central characters and the two works' thematic singleness of purpose. "Parker's Back" has been analyzed to demonstrate its thematic and doctrinal appropriateness as the replacement for the earlier story "The Partridge Festival." Consequently, there remain but five stories to consider in *Everything That Rises Must Converge*. Each of those stories is an integral part of the whole; moreover, though this point need not be argued here, each stands as an example of the American short story as it has developed from Hawthorne and Poe to the present.

In "Greenleaf," the collection's second story, a virtuous, hardworking widow much like Mrs. McIntyre (she too operates a dairy farm), suffers indignity and death as a result of lower-class shiftlessness. Mrs. May has two sons who apparently despise her and each other, and she is clearly envious of her hired man, Mr. Greenleaf, whose sons have risen to prosperity through the kind of hard work her sons scorn. One of her sons is an embittered intellectual and the other is a "nigger insurance man." A scrub bull belonging to the Greenleaf boys gets onto Mrs. May's property, and she fears it will ruin her herd. Thus at the outset of the story sexuality is inherent— animal sexuality, which Mrs. May wishes to restrain for the practical purpose of operating her dairy. The bull grows in importance; eventually Mrs. May imagines him munching away her entire farm. She is described in nonhuman terms: "green rubber curlers sprouted neatly from her forehead and her face beneath them was smooth as concrete with an egg-white paste that drew the wrinkles out while she slept." At the story's opening she dreams of the munching outside her window, and she does not awake until it has reached "her elbow."

Later in the story, "half the night in her sleep she heard a sound as if some large stone were grinding a hole on the outside wall of her brain. She was walking on the inside, over a succession of beautiful rolling hills, planting her stick in front of each step. She became aware after a time that the noise was the sun trying to burn through the tree line and she stopped to watch, safe in the knowledge that it couldn't, that it had to sink the way it always did outside her property" (p. 47). Gradually the sun changes in its shape; it narrows and pales until it looks like a bullet: "Then suddenly it burst through the tree line and raced down the hill toward her." At this point she awakens to the awareness that Greenleaf has released the bull, which she had made him pen up. She determines to force Greenleaf to shoot the animal, and this decision leads to her death and brings the story to its climax.

Recalling Racine's use of the bull and its related imagery in *Phaedra* to embody the Jansenist doctrines of original sin and carnality, one recognizes that Miss O'Connor has imbued the bull in her story with both pagan and Christian significance. In one respect the bull is the dragon which Mrs. May must pass en route to the Father of Souls; in fact, the bull becomes her guide, a maddened creature who buries his head in her lap "like a wild tormented lover." After she is impaled, she continues to stare "straight ahead but the entire scene in front of her had changed—the tree line was a dark wound in a world that was nothing but sky—and she had the look of a person whose sight has been suddenly restored but who finds the light unbearable."

Mrs. May's worst fear has been that she will die and the Greenleafs will acquire her property through her sons' default: they will prove incapable of handling the shiftless, conniving tenant family. Her desire for vindictive and immediate "justice" leads to her death and its concomitant revelation. The instrument of her displacement, the bull, is the symbol of man's fear of carnality, but as the story ends Greenleaf sees her caught on the bull's horns, seeming "to be bent over whispering some last discovery into the animal's ear" (p. 53).

The next story in the collection hinges perfectly on "Greenleaf," for in "A View of the Woods" Mr. Fortune intends to leave all he owns to his granddaughter, whom he believes to be exactly like him because of their physical and temperamental resemblance. However, the old man does not realize that he and the little girl are equally grasping, and he is therefore shocked when she sides with her parents against his selling the "front lawn," a field which affords "a view of the woods." The ferocious child, apparently victorious over the old man, straddles his inert body after they struggle in the dark woods: "The old man looked up into his own image. It was triumphant and hostile. 'You been whipped,' it said, 'by me,' and then it added, bearing down on each word, 'and I'm PURE Pitts.'" Mr. Fortune "managed to roll over and reverse their positions so that he was looking down into the face that was his own." He struck her head against a rock and then, "looking into the face in which the eyes, slowly rolling back, appeared to pay him not the slightest attention, he said, 'There's not an ounce of Pitts in me'" (p. 80).

Like Haze Motes in *Wise Blood,* who thought he was hunting down his conscience and killing it but was actually killing his false self, Mr. Fortune destroys the part of his nature he would repudiate. He loathes his son-in-law, Mary Fortune Pitts's father, and thinks he sees in the child his own moral image as well as his physical image. The story ends with the child's death and the old man's floundering into the newly excavated lake. In the concluding paragraph several of Miss O'Connor's chief images and symbols converge in an arabesque of meaning: "Suddenly the whole lake opened up before him, riding majestically in little corrugated folds toward his feet. He realized suddenly that he could not swim and that he had not bought the boat. On both sides of him he saw that the gaunt trees had thickened into mysterious dark files that were marching across the water and away into the darkness. He looked around desperately for someone to help him but the place was deserted except for one huge yellow monster which sat to the side, as stationary as he was, gorging itself on clay" (p. 81).

The family wished to conserve the line of trees which Mr. Fortune was willing to sacrifice for the sake of progress—a filling station for now and hopefully a whole shopping center, named for him, in the future. The line of trees, associated with revelation and with grace, is underlined in the concluding paragraph, a paraphrase of the biblical source from which Miss O'Connor drew the symbol. When Mr. Fortune sees the trees marching as he drowns, he is, Miss O'Connor wrote, "like the blind man cured in the Gospels, who looked then and saw men as if they were trees, but walking."[4]

The lake itself is important, for Mr. Fortune is responsible for its existence; it marks the recurrence of the destructive but purifying water-force which controls and informs so much of *The Violent Bear It Away*. Other images also enforce Mr. Fortune's self-annihilating baptism. Realizing suddenly that he cannot swim and has not bought the boat, he looks desperately for help but sees nothing save a "huge yellow monster . . . gorging itself on clay." The monster, or dragon, is the bulldozer, which he and Mary Fortune Pitts had watched earlier, relentlessly excavating the earth. It leads one to infer that Mr. Fortune has not made his "mysterious passage" safely but has floundered into the dragon's jaws. However, the marching trees testify to the contrary, as does the fact that the bulldozer gorges itself on clay, the merely physical stuff of man. Mr. Fortune's terrible struggle in the woods has ended in the self-defeat which assures that, for all his faults, grace has descended; murderer or not, he has expiated his sin.

One of Miss O'Connor's most successful stories, "The Enduring Chill," originally published in *Harper's Bazaar* (July 1958) and placed fourth in *Everything That Rises Must Converge*, does not conclude with either death or the foreshadowing of death. Indeed, the comic irony of the story depends upon the central character's living, but he has his revelation nonetheless. Asbury Fox, a self-glorifying would-be artist, returns home to his mother's Georgia farm, determined to die leaving behind his one completed manuscript—a long letter, complete with literary allusions—to torture his mother for her supposed smothering of his talents.

In the end Asbury learns that he is not to die and that his disobeying his mother by drinking unpasteurized milk is the cause of his illness. He has undulant fever, which the country doctor tells him is "the same as Bang's in a cow," thus explaining (as Hyman points out in his *Flannery O'Connor*, p. 27) Asbury's feelings for "a small, wall-eyed Guernsey . . . watching him steadily as if she sensed some bond between them." At the announcement of the nature of

Asbury's disease, his mother says, "It'll keep coming back but it won't kill you."

In the final paragraph Asbury sees that his eyes look paler: "They looked shocked clean as if they had been prepared for some awful vision about to come down on him." Miss O'Connor's description of the setting reiterates her symbols of grace, by now familiar: "a blinding red-gold sun moved serenely from under a purple cloud." It includes her most explicit statement of the meaning of the line of trees: "The treeline was black against the crimson sky. It formed a brittle wall, standing as if it were the frail defense he had set up in his mind to protect him from what was coming" (p. 114). Shortly thereafter she writes that the "old life in him was exhausted. He awaited the coming of the new." Rarely does she so specify the moment of Christian rebirth—the death of the old and the emergence of the new in Christ.

As always, the image of grace arises from within the story in terms of its details; it is not imposed from outside. Earlier, Asbury had dwelt upon a water stain on the ceiling; it looked like a "fierce bird with spread wings" and "with an icicle crosswise in his beak. The story concludes: "The fierce bird which through the years of his childhood and the days of his illness had been poised over his head, waiting mysteriously, appeared all at once to be in motion. Asbury blanched and the last film of illusion was torn as if by a whirlwind from his eyes. He saw that for the rest of his days, frail, racked but enduring, he would live in face of a purifying terror. A feeble cry, a last impossible protest escaped him. But the Holy Ghost, emblazoned in ice instead of fire, continued, implacable, to descend" (p. 114).

Asbury's victory is in his total defeat: he has nothing left, not even the romantic self-pity which had made death seem delicious. His interview with a priest, largely another means to shock his Protestant mother, had been a failure; the priest took his attitudinizing not at all seriously, lecturing him instead on his ignorance of the catechism. Here, incidentally, Hyman is in error when he assumes the Church to be one of Miss O'Connor's satirical targets. The priest is blind in one eye and deaf in one ear, but these symbolic failings are used positively here as elsewhere in Miss O'Connor's work. The single eye of the owl in *Wise Blood* closes when Haze affirms "I AM clean." Matthew tells us that "The light of the body is the eye: if therefore, thine eye be single, thy whole body shall be full of light" (Matt. 6:22). Later the one-eyed bear, victim of the hawk's pelleting, affirms the same theological concept. Furthermore, Rayber in *The Violent Bear It Away* is deafened by a shotgun blast, but his hearing aid makes Bishop's cries seem to come from inside him. Physical handicaps do not necessarily represent spiritual failings for an author, one of whose heroes (Haze Motes) must blind himself before he can "see."

Just as Asbury's contact with the Church fails, so does his effort to establish secular communion with his mother's Negro servants. He calls for the Negroes to say goodbye because he wishes to hurt his mother and because he relishes the image of the dying young man taking leave of his unlettered but faithful friends. The Negroes are notably dishonest in their conversation with the sick man, arguing together about how fine he looks. One is offended because Asbury gives the other a package of cigarettes; all in all, his humanist substitute for a meaningful relationship, his phony liberalism, proves a miserable failure. Earlier he had cultivated the Negroes in order to write a play about them. In the dairy his defiance of his mother (drinking the milk and smoking) thinly disguises his own inadequacy while revealing his ignorance of the dairy's operation.

Asbury Fox sees himself clearly at the conclusion of "The Enduring Chill." The whirlwind tears the "last film of illusion . . . from his eyes," and he faces not death but life without the protection of his age or of its secularism, both of which obscure man's oneness with God. Just as O. E. Parker must die for Obadiah Elihue Parker to be born, so must Asbury die in sin to be reborn in grace.

"The Comforts of Home," first published in *Kenyon Review* (Fall 1960) and placed fifth in *Everything That Rises*, dramatizes the death of a do-gooder mother who has taken a "moral moron," a nymphomaniac, into her home despite the protests of her son, Thomas, a complacent writer of local history. Thomas fears and despises Sara Hamm, alias Star Drake, for he recognizes her as "the very stuff of corruption, but blameless corruption because there was no responsible faculty behind it." Looking at the "most unendurable form of innocence," he absently asks himself what "the attitude of God was to this, meaning if possible to adopt it."

More sophisticated than Enoch Emery in *Wise Blood,* Thomas nevertheless gives in to his own daddy's wise blood by permitting the voice of his dead father, whom he had despised, to dictate to him the means of ridding himself and his mother of the girl. He is ineffectual and knows it, but there is something about the girl's face that suggests "the blindness of those who don't know they cannot see." Frustrated by his failure to force his mother to turn the girl out, Thomas exults when he discovers Sara has stolen his revolver. He reports the theft to the sheriff, who promises to search the girl's room and arrest her if the gun is found. At home, awaiting the sheriff, Thomas discovers the gun is back in its place; his father's voice, which has established itself in Thomas's head, counsels him to hide the weapon in Sara's purse, but he hesitates until it is too late and she sees him. Again taking his cues from the inner voice, Thomas first claims that he found the gun in Sara's bag and then, in the voice of his father, shouts, "The dirty criminal slut stole my gun." "His mother gasped at the sound of the other presence in his voice."

Thomas's moral complacency, his smug self-satisfaction, is all but over with the emergence of the "other presence in his voice." The story ends rapidly: the girl lunges at Thomas, and the mother springs between the two just as the old man yells his last command—"Fire!" "The blast was like a sound meant to bring an end to evil in the world. Thomas heard it as a sound that would shatter the laughter of sluts until all shrieks were stilled and nothing was left to disturb the peace of perfect order" (p. 141). But of course the shot has no such effect: Thomas's mother, not Sara, is killed, and the sheriff sees "the facts as if they were already in print: the fellow had intended all along to kill his mother and pin it on the girl." The sheriff has a further insight as he sees "the killer and the slut . . . about to collapse into each other's arms": "The sheriff knew a nasty bit when he saw it. He was accustomed to enter upon scenes not as bad as he had hoped to find them, but this one met his expectations" (p. 142).

This is one story in *Everything That Rises* which Stanley Edgar Hyman considers "a mistake from the beginning." He says it travesties the familiar "triad of parent-child-intruder" (*Flannery O'Connor,* p. 28), but he does not support his notion that it is a travesty. Without arguing with Hyman's value judgment, one must protest that the story is thematically not a mistake for the collection:

Thomas's rising and his eventual converging are made possible by the failure of his intended Godlike destruction of evil in the world. Because he is only human, he proves incapable of adopting God's attitude toward "the stuff of corruption" and yields instead to the moral techniques of his father—and with fatal results. His mother is dead and the comforts of home are lost forever; more important, Thomas who had insisted that his mother's pity of the delinquent girl was misplaced, is now in the role of the killer, and the lustful killer at that, collapsing into the arms of the slut.

The beauty of "The Comforts of Home" is that the terrible conclusion, which meets the evil-minded sheriff's expectation, is all of Thomas's making: his self-righteous detestation of the girl's moral failings and his desire to leave "nothing to disturb the peace of perfect order" reveal that he seeks external progress and earthly utopia. Because the terms of human existence are not "perfect order," his expectations are not realized; instead, his world is turned upside down as he assumes the role of criminal, sharing the guilt of "the stuff of corruption," at least in the eyes of men. In theological terms his crime is pride, and it is that pride which brings him down, not Sara Hamm.

In "Revelation," the seventh story in the collection, Mrs. Turpin is struck on the head by a book savagely hurled by a sick girl in the doctor's waiting room. Mr. Turpin has just said, "If it's one thing I am, it's grateful. When I think who all I could have been besides myself and what all I got, a little of everything, and a good disposition besides, I just feel like shouting, 'Thank you, Jesus, for making everthing the way it is.'" Mrs. Turpin takes the girl's attack and later denunciation as a sign; she feels that she has been singled out for a "message," but she cannot understand why she is called an "old wart hog from hell" when there is "trash" there, to whom, as she thinks, the "message" "might justly have been applied."

At the height of her resistance and repudiation of the "message," Mrs. Turpin demands to know "how" she is a hog. Standing at her farm pig-parlor, she addresses God, though she never speaks His name. She says, "If you like trash better, go get yourself some trash then. You could have made me trash. Or a nigger. If trash is what you wanted why didn't you make me trash?" A moment later, "in the deepening light" in which "everything was taking a mysterious hue,

. . . She braced herself for a final assault and this time her voice rolled out over the pasture. 'Go on,' she yelled, 'call me a hog! Call me a hog again. From hell. Call me a wart hog from hell. Put that bottom rail on top. There'll still be a top and bottom!' A garbled echo returned to her. A final surge of fury shook her and she roared, 'Who do you think you are?' " (p. 216).

Mrs. Turpin's "message" has begun the process of upending her values, and the process is completed in the revelation with which the story ends. Her question, "Who do you think you are?" carried "over the pasture and across the highway and the cotton field and returned to her clearly like an answer from beyond the wood." Bent over the pig-parlor fence, she studies the hogs which seem "to pant with a secret life" while she seems to be "absorbing some abysmal life-giving knowledge." When she raises her head, she sees a purple streak in the sky, "cutting through a field of crimson and leading, like an extension of the highway, into the descending dusk." Then she sees the streak in the sky becoming "a vast swinging bridge" extending "upward from the earth through a field of living fire." "Upon it a vast horde of souls were rumbling toward heaven. There were whole companies of white-trash, clean for the first time in their lives, and bands of black niggers in white robes, and battalions of freaks and lunatics shouting and clapping and leaping like frogs. And bringing up the end of the procession was a tribe of people whom she recognized at once as those who, like herself and Claud, had always had a little of everything and the God-given wit to use it right." Mrs. Turpin leans forward to "observe them closer" and discovers that her own kind are "marching behind the others with great dignity, accountable as they had always been for good order and common sense and respectable behavior." She notices that only her kind are singing on key, "yet she could see by their shocked and altered faces that even their virtues were being burned away" (p. 217). At the moment of her most violent pride—the challenging question "Who do you think you are?"—the ironic answer of who she herself is has been provided.

Mrs. Turpin's revelation is implicit in the other stories in *Everything That Rises*. In "The Lame Shall Enter First" Sheppard begins to experience the burning away of his virtues as the story closes. In "Parker's Back" O. E. Parker's vision leads to his impractical desire for a "picture of God." In "Judgement Day" old Tanner, miserable in New York, realizes that he should have swallowed his pride and operated his and Coleman's still for the "nigger" Dr. Foley. In "The Comforts of Home" Thomas's desire for "perfect order" leads to the total disordering of his life. In "The Enduring Chill" Asbury Fox's sense of his uniqueness and superiority leads to the frail and racked condition which he will endure in the face of a "purifying terror." In "A View of the Woods" Mr. Fortune's "identical-eye-to-identical-eye" struggle with Mary Fortune Pitts leads to both of their deaths but takes him past the dragon.

In both the title story and "Greenleaf," a complacent, middle-class woman's values are upended in a violent prelude to her death. In "Everything That Rises" Julian's mother insists that she "knows who she is," but the Negro woman, wearing a hat exactly like hers, presents a "negative image" similar to the one Coleman's face shows Tanner in "Judgement Day." Unfortunately, before she dies, Julian's mother does not recognize her kinship with the Negro woman, but the story ends hopefully with Julian's imminent "entry to the world of guilt and sorrow." The scrub bull which destroys Mrs. May in "Greenleaf" serves to reveal the fatuity of her pretended superiority and her concern with material values. The bull is a "patient god come down to woo her," but, strangely, it is also associated with the shiftless, ignorant Greenleaf and his faith-healing wife. Mrs. May's vengeful determination to make Greenleaf shoot his sons' bull comes after he has witnessed her own sons' violent, hateful squabbling.

The "patient god come down to woo" Mrs. May is associated also with the suffering Christ, for the line of trees behind the bull looks like a "dark wound"; her recovery of sight makes clear that in the convergence of death—occurring, incredibly, on the horns of the bull she had intended to have destroyed—Mrs. May has risen above secular pride. Bleakly she had realized that the Greenleaf boys (married to French wives) would eventually constitute "society," and she had complacently compared her life of hard work to Mrs. Greenleaf's wallowing on the ground over buried newspaper clippings, the "demented" woman's ritual of faith healing. "Before any kind of judgement seat, she would be able to say: I've worked, I have not wallowed" (p. 51).

Such testimony, however, is of no avail before the judgment seat about which Miss O'Connor writes. As in the case of Mrs. Turpin in "Revelation," Mrs. May's hard work is irrelevant. Her fear that her sons will yield the farm to the Greenleaf boys is doubtless prophetic, and even if the Greenleaf boys and their parents do not represent "society," their children, schooled in the convent and speaking French as well as "Greenleaf" English, will. Mrs. May's ironically appropriate death and the hint of her vision which transcends respectability offer her only hope.

Throughout the stories in *Everything That Rises Must Converge,* loss of self-sufficiency, of pride of station, and of possessions functions to alter worldly vision and replace it with a higher vision. Just as Mrs. May sees the world differently at the end, so does Julian's mother undergo a change in vision. Her regression to childhood is a hopeful sign, as is the fact that one eye, "large and staring, moved slightly to the left as if it had become unmoored," while the other "remained fixed on [Julian], raked his face again, found nothing and closed." Julian's secularism has no meaning, no answer for her at the crossroads, for her single eye of vision is unmoored from secular sights. But her altered vision precipitates a change in Julian's world, a change marked by the cluster of lights which "drifted further away the faster he ran."

The Specter of Death Banished

Recourse to biographical facts about Miss O'Connor's last years reveals little of literary importance, though the story of her struggle for life and her acceptance of death is a heroic one. Robert Fitzgerald has told the story well in his introduction to the posthumous collection; perhaps his terse quotation from one of Miss O'Connor's letters says it best: "Ask Sally to pray the lupus don't finish me off too quick" (p. xxv). The writer, for whom death was a brother to the imagination, did not seek her friend's prayers merely that she might have a few additional months of life; she sought to live to complete the work she had begun.

The collection was uppermost in her mind, and she made decisions regarding its content after the final illness set in. As Fitzgerald tells us, she spent a great part of 1964 in Atlanta's Piedmont Hospital, and, suffering a kidney failure in July after her return to Andalusia, she died at a Milledgeville hospital on August 3. But the collection was complete, grace note and all; only Fitzgerald's warm and appreciative introduction remained to be written—a grace note of another sort since the Fitzgeralds had known and encouraged Miss O'Connor almost from the start of her professional career.

At the time of her death Miss O'Connor's critical reputation was increasing; her stories had won first prizes in the O. Henry competitions of 1956 and 1963, and both "Revelation" and "Parker's Back" in the last collection were to rival the title story in popularity and critical approval. The novels would continue to raise difficult questions—and some eyebrows—and the judgment that she belongs with those storytellers unable to handle the longer form remains a debated question. However, her pervasive art and the total unity of her published work will doubtless continue to win readers for all the collected stories as well as the novels.

Miss O'Connor's first collection was about travelers, but they were moving horizontally, for the most part. One is tempted to interpret the collection as providing what Philip Wheelwright posits as a vertical bar in human experience. Complaining that Cartesian thought has bifurcated human experience on a horizontal plane, Wheelwright schematizes his concept as follows: on a horizontal bar, E, or ego (experiencer), knows P or phenomena, "partly as experience and . . . partly as a contributor to their connection and significance."[5] Meantime, a vertical bar arises from C, community, and goes upward to M, myth or mystery. Wheelwright's C could stand as well for communion, and if Miss O'Connor had been familiar with his idea, she would doubtless have substituted communion of saints for community.

As we noted earlier, one story in *A Good Man Is Hard to Find* deals with vertical, not horizontal, motion. In "A Stroke of Good Fortune" Ruby Hill's ascent of her apartment house steps brings her to the meaning of life as it necessarily relates to the mystery of death. She had hoped to remain young by avoiding childbearing, but with awareness of the stir of life within her she begins to comprehend the magnitude of life's mystery. In "Judgement Day," as old Tanner descends the stairs in his daughter's apartment house, he experiences a truly transcendent vision; the full meaning of his vision strongly suggests that in the final collection Flannery O'Connor had come at last to recognize the relevance of social and racial relations to the larger issues of faith. Ruby Hill moved upward to mystery, breaking the hold of the purely empirical upon her; though old Tanner moved downward to a fuller sense of communion with men, his experience also achieves the upward and converging movement implicit in the collection.

"Everything That Rises Must Converge" ends in suspended horizontal movement, Julian's failure to move toward the goal which lies before him in space. The title story and the concluding story, "Judgement Day," are the only two in the collection which focus on Negro-white relations, specifically, the convergence of the two races as the Negro rises socially and economically.

"Judgement Day," which rounds out the frame for the collection, is the appropriate final word from an artist whose recurrent theme was her belief that salvation is for sinners and that (contrary to Haze Motes's assertion) the fall requires redemption and the two make inevitable a final judgment. This grace note is by no means a tacked-on blessing, a theological coda: it is simply a more directly stated affirmation of the redemption than Miss O'Connor usually permitted herself. After the critical haze which met *Wise Blood* she was determined to draw larger, clearer pictures for her "compassion-dulled" audience of unbelievers and passive assenters. This clarification is achieved in the stories in *Everything That Rises Must Converge*: from the title story onward, she returns to her themes of sorrow and guilt, man's futile movement through physical space and historical time, and she progresses constantly toward her eternal crossroads.

Perhaps the greatest difference between the final collection and the earlier works is that by 1961 Miss O'Connor had a name for that crossroads: she had begun to read the works of Teilhard de Chardin and must have recognized that his "point omega" was precisely the goal toward which she, as Christian and as writer, was moving. In her own life the communion of saints helped her to prepare for the "good death in Christ." In her art she sought to provide a basis of communion, a community in time and space which shared the history of the South and of mankind, chiefly as recorded in the Old and New Testaments; furthermore, with no lessening of her faith in a personal redemption, she had found in Teilhard a richer vision. His work, arising from experimental science, affirmed her belief in an evolving universe—a universe in which the constant (even if slow) movement is upward toward a point of universal convergence. For both Teilhard and Miss O'Connor such a convergence coincides with another mystical transformation: the world made one and perfectly expressive of the risen Christ.

It appears more than fortuitous that in their final literary statements Miss O'Connor and Teilhard affirmed the same belief and, moreover, the same scriptural passage. In "Judgement Day" old Tanner, from Corinth, Georgia, has a vision of the last judgment that brings to mind one of the Gospels' most stirring affirmations of Christ's victory over death. In his final testimony, part of the conclusion of *The Future of Man*, Teilhard quotes the same passage (1 Cor. 15:26–28) under the heading "What I Believe":

> The last enemy that shall be destroyed is death. For he hath put all things under his feet. But when he saith, all things are put under him, it is manifest that he is excepted, which did put all things under him.
>
> And when all things shall be subdued unto him, then shall the Son also himself be subject unto him that put all things under him, that God may be all in all.
>
> 7 April 1955[6]

Elsewhere, speaking of the incarnation, the Christian's concept of God's entry into the world of matter, Teilhard seems to echo the same passage in what is possibly his most direct statement of belief: "Having thus established Himself at the heart of matter, He takes over the direction of evolution. When He has gathered everything in, He will close in again upon Himself and on His conquest."[7]

Miss O'Connor's use of the name Corinth, combined with other suggestive details in "Judgement Day," supports the belief that she returned to her earlier story with the express purpose of affirming the same scriptural truth Teilhard quotes. She may not have known this part of Teilhard's work, of course, for the passage from Corinthians is important to most Christians, Protestant as well as Catholic; nevertheless, at the end of her life, Miss O'Connor's art and Teilhard's thought seem to have converged in a literary expression of the same fundamental belief.

Few critics recognize the true nature of Miss O'Connor's use of Teilhard's ideas. This point is illustrated, in part at least, by Marion Montgomery's claim that Miss O'Connor "opposes Teilhard's reading of evil," though he admits that she "never spoke in direct opposition to Teilhard."[8] Though his argument is well constructed, Montgomery fails to observe that Miss O'Connor's Devil (a being in whom she most certainly believed) always assumes flesh in wholly credible, naturalistic details, whether as a mechanized dragon or as a roaring lion. Teilhard's noosphere is the province of thought toward which, he argues, the universe is moving, and Miss O'Connor, for all the external, even shocking, action of her stories, is largely concerned with that province also. Over and over, an inner voice materializes into an external form: Tarwater's friend, for instance, and Haze Motes's preoccupation with Jesus, a shadowy figure at the back of his mind.

As Catholics, Miss O'Connor and Teilhard shared a basically incarnational vision; for them, anagogical truth was both naturalistic and mystical, for the creation continues to partake of God. Neither writer divided the world into idea and reality; both recognized the interpenetration of the real and the ideal. Their phenomenological tendencies permitted subjective experience full equality with the empirical. Such a reading of the world, including evil, disturbs the modern mind almost as much as it excites it.

Teilhard disturbed his readers from the start by his deployment of scientifically impeccable data to serve metaphysical ends. Miss O'Connor disturbs through her refusal to equate physical suffering and death with evil; in her stories "rising" has little to do with our normal sense of improvement. Readers would be less disturbed if they recognized that, for both writers, the external is but a sign of the internal and that events have their meaning in individual consciousness.

Montgomery's article ends with the warning that one should "hesitate to conclude that [Miss O'Connor] implies [Teilhard's] vision as a resolution of the mystery of the tragedy she presents" in "Everything That Rises Must Converge" ("O'Connor and Teilhard," p. 42); to do so, he says, would be to use Teilhard's thought as a *deus ex machina*. He argues that this story, in which Miss O'Connor specifically "refers to Teilhard and his 'spectacle of the divine ascent of creation,'" is essentially a tragedy: "the main character, rising through what he supposes a superior intellect, is defeated out of his blind pride." To enforce the point about tragedy, he adds that the character also "recognizes his parentage at the end." The comparison with Oedipus simply will not do here, at least as Montgomery presents it, for Miss O'Connor nowhere suggests that Julian is rising through his superior intellect; she makes him ludicrous and ineffectual throughout. Furthermore, if he recognizes a parent at the end, that recognition is less important than his dislocation in time and space, which parallels his mother's reversion, at death, to an earlier and (for her) happier time.

Montgomery would have done better to regard the story as another "Mauriac prologue" in which the operation of matter produces a bona fide revelation for one character and prepares another for grace. Miss O'Connor's use of the ticklish racial elements suggests her recognition, with Teilhard, that though man is subdivided into races, he is now tending toward greater, not less, unity. Like Tanner and Coleman in "Judgement Day," Julian's mother and the Negress are brought together through external details, which Julian at least is able to recognize. Such an interpretation is wholly compatible with Teilhard's "spectacle of the divine ascent of creation" and with Miss O'Connor's often reiterated belief in the anagogical method. Her orthodoxy confirms that Julian's eventual entry to the world of guilt and sorrow prepares him for grace and redemption.

Unfortunately, Montgomery's reading of "Everything That Rises Must Converge" disavows the story's comic nature. Julian is no Oedipus, and his mother is certainly no Jocasta. Julian is a poseur throughout, and his mother is a pious hypocrite whose death is no more tragic than is Hulga's loss of her leg in "Good Country People." Death need not be elevated to the tragic to achieve profound implications; indeed, the comic experience nearly always provides insights more profound than characters or readers anticipate. As comic characters Julian and his mother may be observed from outside in all their weakness and silliness.

Teilhard and Miss O'Connor place convergence at a similar spot. For Teilhard it is the point omega, the peak of the cone created by man's gradual rising; the point has its own consciousness, but all other consciousnesses participate in it. It is a point which is becoming; it is the object of all consciousness and of all growth. For Miss O'Connor the point of convergence is realization, another word for growth, though wholly limited to mind. For both writers convergence occurs out of time, or at least outside the usual horizontal time of history. But convergence is nevertheless a product of time, seen as the events of history themselves. Hence Miss O'Connor's convergences are both naturalistic and mystical; they point to the divine life and our participation in it.

Miss O'Connor's most notable single image in "Everything That Rises Must Converge" is Julian's final displacement, his entrapment on the treadmill of events, which holds him suspended between cause and effect. To judge Julian's treatment of his mother is beside the point, for its effect is clear; his experience culminates on the treadmill, not in a specific "good" or "evil" act. His consciousness—and the reader's—is the real arena of action. Teilhard's point omega similarly transcends mere causality; that is what transcendence means. The creation of a thinking universe demands material participation, but at the point of convergence there is no cause or effect —only unity. Neither Teilhard nor Miss O'Connor seeks to resolve the basic human problem; neither seeks to deny the fact of evil. Rather, both recognize that man's sphere is the mundane and that it is adequate for the divine purpose.

All the critics have followed Fitzgerald's lead in his introduction to *Everything That Rises Must Converge,* and apparently all (with one important exception) agree with him that Miss O'Connor took her title from Teilhard "with full respect and with a profound and necessary irony (p. xxx). Rarely, however, has a critic attempted to define that irony, or, for that matter, to spell out precisely how Teilhard's work affected Miss O'Connor's fiction.

It is no accident that Teilhard's *The Future of Man* speaks of the arrival at what he calls the crossroads, where men must contribute "courage and resourcefulness . . . in overcoming the forces of isolationism, even of repulsion, which seem to drive them apart rather than draw them together" (pp. 72–73). In chapter four, "Some Reflections on Progress," Teilhard argues in support of the "growth of consciousness" (p. 64)—awareness of the progress of life through synthesis—which brings him to the crossroads. The roads toward progress through unification are two: external and internal, compulsion and unanimity. (Interestingly, these terms parallel exactly those Mauriac used in his denial of André Gide's secularism.)

In part two of the same essay Teilhard, admitting human divergence between those whose hopes are spiritual and those whose hopes are material, maintains nevertheless that "any two forces, provided both are positive, must *a priori* be capable of growth by merging together" (pp. 76–77). Hence "A Principle of Convergence" argues that there is a growth of the universe: "the gradual concentration of its physico-chemical elements in nuclei of increasing complexity, each succeeding stage of material concentration and differentiation being accompanied by a more advanced form of spontaneity and spiritual energy" (p. 78).

Miss O'Connor's "Everything That Rises Must Converge" dramatizes precisely this proposition: although Julian apparently does not rise or converge, his faith in external, compulsory unification of the races "grows" through his confrontation with the mystery of death and his necessity to overcome physical space in order to find his way back to a world of guilt and sorrow. The story clearly implies that his emergence into that world will be "accompanied by a more advanced form of spontaneity and spiritual energy." Not only will he have achieved greater vision for himself, but his vision will far exceed that of his mother and the Negro woman who has been her fateful adversary.

Julian's gain, or growth, must be reckoned in terms of spiritual energy activated at his "peculiar crossroads"; his consciousness will be expanded at a particular coinciding of space and time. Such expansion, according to Teilhard, is the goal of life; Miss O'Connor's suggestion of that experience is intense, for she leaves Julian running in place, straining toward a cluster of lights which recede from him as he runs. In *The Future of Man* Teilhard declares that man is enabled "to banish the spectre of Death . . . by the idea . . . that ahead of, or rather in the heart of, a universe prolonged along its axis of complexity, there exists a divine centre of convergence, the point omega," from which "there constantly emanate radiations hitherto only perceptible to those persons whom we call 'mystics' " (p. 122).

The concept of the "point omega," the "divine centre of convergence," is the key to Miss O'Connor's affinity for the thought of her scientific contemporary. Nor is the concept a surprising one to find in the works of two of the most intensely Catholic writers in the recent past. It is such a belief, for instance, which permitted Thomas

Stearns Eliot, among other religious writers, to affirm the salutory nature of "positive evil." In "The Second Coming" William Butler Yeats recognized that "the best lack all conviction, while the worst/ Are full of passionate intensity." Much earlier, William Blake had glorified the power and virility of the Devil's party and in his prophetic book *Milton* had sought to enlist even the Great Puritan into that communion. Whereas the Anglo-Catholic C. S. Lewis has recently sought to effect a divorce of the opposites wed in Blake's *Marriage of Heaven and Hell,* Miss O'Connor and Teilhard testify that the marriage is not final. In short, Miss O'Connor came to a realization, not wholly compatible with Mauriac's views, that for all the value of internal as opposed to external progress, the universe and man are such that even mere humanist-oriented concern with appearance and social welfare may provide a "positive [force] capable of growth by merging" with spiritual values at the point omega.

In several ways Miss O'Connor's final collection is a strange one for a writer whose earliest example had been François Mauriac, for not only does she incorporate an increasing number of secular concerns in her fiction but she also brings her readers to the very point of realizing grace; no longer are all her stories prologues in the sense that they intimate revelations without dramatizing them. In "The Enduring Chill," for instance, she dramatizes, as few writers since the seventeenth-century metaphysicals have done, the full mystery and terror of the descent of the Holy Ghost. It is gratifying that a Jesuit critic, John J. Burke, noted as early as 1966 that in the final three stories in *Everything That Rises Must Converge* ("Revelation," "Parker's Back," and "Judgement Day"), one finds "a spiritually converging world where the universal domination of Christ, as an intrinsic energy, has acquired an urgency and intensity."[9]

Father Burke is the only critic who seems to have challenged the general assumption that Miss O'Connor's use of Teilhard's ideas for her title was ironic. He is clearly on the right track when he suggests examination of the ordering of the final three stories to determine where Miss O'Connor assumed convergence would occur. Unfortunately, however, Father Burke's view is too restricted, for the final story relates directly to the title story in content and in emphasis upon social convergence. Hence, as we have emphasized, the total collection (not only the last three stories) is ordered for thematic purposes.

Julian's plight in the title story is resolved with Tanner's vision of the last judgment; the resolution, incorporating a sense of the oneness of men and the common failing of all flesh, is essentially spiritual. Though Julian never recognizes his real similarity to the Negroes he patronizes in his smug liberalism, Tanner recognizes himself in the Negro Coleman, his "negative image," "as if clownishness and captivity had been their common lot."

Julian postpones "from moment to moment his entry into the world of guilt and sorrow"; hence the emphasis in the title story is upon man's entrance to existential time. He is at the brink of what Robert Penn Warren calls the "convulsion of the world" and the "awful responsibility of time."[10] Like Warren in one sense, Miss O'Connor seeks in all her work to discover personal identity through awareness of man's place in history: the difference lies in the fact that history, for her, is even more immense than for Warren.

The coffin-dreams in Miss O'Connor's earlier fiction, with their oppressive sense of captivity supported by images of caged animals, come to their logical Christian and eschatological conclusion in the breaking open of the coffin old Tanner thinks is bearing him home to native soil for burial. (For the primitive Christian, history is of no real import, for the last judgment is imminent; similarly, the Jews cherish a long tradition of belief in the end of mundane affairs when they will all be caught up and returned to the Holy Land.) That Tanner's dream of resurrection is, ironically, false does not matter, for he is freed from all worldly distinctions; in Teilhard's words he reaches the crossroads and contributes "courage and resourcefulness . . . in overcoming the forces of isolationism, even of repulsion, which seem to drive [men] apart."

The reader recognizes—uncomfortably, no doubt, if he is dedicated to the liberal "cause"—that it is the Negro actor who is enchained, held by his sense of identity and isolated from union with other people; he is obliged to deny his faith as he denies human relationships, all for the sake of superficial "equality." Tanner opens his eyes at the climax of his vision and is shocked that "this nigger ain't Coleman," his "negative image" and spiritual comrade.

Man's captivity, symbolized and dramatized in all Miss O'Connor's works, ends only with death, and in "Judgement Day" she permits the reader a glimpse of the "rising and converging" in death, which was the end and meaning of Teilhard's analysis of psychological and biological evolution. One recalls again that Teilhard regarded belief in "a divine centre of convergence" as man's means of banishing "the spectre of death." For Teilhard, even the machine, the humanist's terror, is evolving with man toward a synthesis of the divine will. Flannery O'Connor's use of Rayber's hearing aid and the transfer truck in *The Violent Bear It Away* and of the bulldozer in "A View of the Woods" suggests that she was fully aware of the extent to which machines serve as emblems of the way past the dragon en route to the Father of Souls. In "The River" Mr. Paradise is at once an "ancient water monster" and an emblem of man's reliance upon the mechanical. Nevertheless, he makes it possible for the child to go under the river, dying the perfect death of innocence and faith. Finally the boy "knew he was getting somewhere."

In another, perhaps fortuitous way—his name—Mr. Paradise is related to the final collection, for Julian's postponing his entry to existential time places the thoughtful reader in the moment of eternal oneness between eviction from the garden (*Paradise Lost*) and the passage of the dragon (*Paradise Regained*). Julian begins the struggle and old Tanner is victorious; the way back to paradise is upward at the point omega where everything converges—Tanner's success in his friendship with Coleman as well as the failure of Julian and the Negroes on the bus.

Miss O'Connor's revision of "The Geranium" supports the belief in her increasing affinity for Teilhard's principle of convergence, for the story originally did no more than dramatize an old man's loneliness in alien country. The revision partakes of the "huge and *totally* human hope" of which Teilhard writes in the epilogue to *The Divine Milieu*.

Teilhard's unification of "fundamental Christian vision and scientific knowledge" was probably the culminating influence upon Miss O'Connor's treatment of her South and of her people. Among Father de Chardin's "earliest mystical intimations," according to the Harper and Row translation of *The Future of Man*, occurs this statement: "At its inception an operation of a transcendent order was required, grafting—in accordance with mysterious but physically regulated conditions—the Person of a Deity on to the Human Cosmos" (p. 304). The creative imagination—unable, as Miss O'Connor so often observed, to deal with abstractions of faith or of any other human condition—would naturally transmute a statement of this sort, treating it at once in its most literal and most metaphysical sense. This is the transformational act of the poet who wrenches a word from its hackneyed context back to the vigor of a primary meaning. Teilhard's "grafting of the Person of a Deity on to the Human Cosmos" almost certainly became O. E. Parker's acquisition of a tattoo of Christ on his back, totally alienating him from his world and serving as the beginning of a transcendent order for him. The editor of *The Future of Man* notes that this idea of Teilhard was "set forth in *La Vie Cosmique* as early as 1916" (p. 304). This fact makes academic the question of whether Miss O'Connor actually saw the 1964 edition of *The Future of Man* before writing "Parker's Back." Apparently Teilhard's ideas were pervasive and continuous, and Miss O'Connor, partly through shared faith and partly through reading his work, arrived at essentially the same Christology.

Links between characters and situations in both collections and both novels recur frequently, as Mrs. Brittain has noted in "The Fictional Family of Flannery O'Connor." Perhaps the most striking similarity is Haze Motes's coffin-dream ending with his waking to see the "Parrum nigger," the porter he thinks grew up in Eastrod, and Tanner's liberating coffin-dream ending with his waking to see the inimical, if not diabolical, Negro actor. In *Wise Blood* the porter voices his denial sourly and triumphantly and offers no aid to the sick man who wishes to escape his confinement; in "Judgement Day" the denial is more violent, for the actor says, "Ain't no judgement day." Instead of helping him, the actor thrusts Tanner's head and arms through the banister rails and hangs him over the stairwell "like a man in the stocks." The speech pattern of the actor, especially in his regression here and in his terms of abuse for Tanner, suggests that he is actually what Tanner thinks him to be—"a nigger from back home."

Julian's mother in "Everything That Rises Must Converge" also dies as a result of an outrage at the hands of a Negro, a woman who knocks her down. Part of the impact of the story lies in Julian's mother's conviction that she "knows who she is," despite the obvious fact that the world around her has changed drastically and no longer represents the values she endorses; however, the full import of the story clearly depends upon what we learn about Julian and his reaction to his mother's death. She regresses to childhood just before her death, whereas Tanner in the concluding story progresses to the ultimate vision of equality, which knows no physical standards and depends on a self-knowledge entirely different from hers.

Though the doctrinal progression of the stories is linear, its force is in their upward movement. The first and last stories have been examined here in details of plot and character, but enough has been said to suggest the necessity of viewing the entire final collection as an entity, rather than as a series of tour de force productions calculated to titillate or to impress with their individual virtuosity. Miss O'Connor continued in her final collection to testify to the central experience in her life, the Christian faith which she recognized as lacking committed, much less violent, adherents. That lack—given her belief in spiritual progress, which is also at the heart of Teilhard de Chardin's writings—became for her yet another condition of salvation, a means of preparing the ground for spiritual awakening.

The Violent Bear It Away concludes with Francis Marion Tarwater's vision of paradise and his joining the communion of saints: "a line of men whose lives were chosen to sustain [his hunger], who would wander in the world, strangers from that violent country where the silence is never broken except to shout the truth." He hears his great commission: "GO WARN THE CHILDREN OF GOD OF THE TERRIBLE SPEED OF MERCY. The words were as silent as seeds opening one at a time in his blood."

Notes

Chapter One

[1] Miss O'Connor wrote four books of fiction: *Wise Blood* (New York: Harcourt, Brace, 1952), *A Good Man Is Hard to Find* (New York: Harcourt, Brace, 1955), *The Violent Bear It Away* (New York: Farrar, Straus & Cudahy, 1960), and *Everything That Rises Must Converge* (New York: Farrar, Straus & Giroux, 1965). *Everything That Rises Must Converge* and *Flannery O'Connor, Mystery and Manners: Occasional Prose* (New York: Farrar, Straus & Giroux, 1969) appeared posthumously. Sally and Robert Fitzgerald selected and edited the work for *Mystery and Manners,* and Fitzgerald's introduction to *Everything That Rises* contains the best biographical essay in print. All of Miss O'Connor's writings, both imaginative and critical, appear in the bibliography of this study; initial periodical as well as book publication is indicated.

[2] Quoted by William Van O'Connor in *Esprit* 8 (Winter 1964): 37.

[3] *Critic* 21 (June–July 1963): 29.

[4] Harvey C. Webster gave Miss O'Connor's *Wise Blood* its only favorable review. Recognizing that "all the characters are symbols, like Kafka's K or, more exactly, like the salesman in Wilder's *Heaven's My Destination,*" he described *Wise Blood* as "an excellent first novel—both a promise and an achievement" ("Nihilism As a Faith," *New Leader* [23 June 1952]: 23). This judgment is in sharp contrast to those of most other critics, who saw only freaks and grotesques.

[5] "Lewis and O'Connor: Prophets of the Added Dimension" (review of *Letters* of C. S. Lewis, ed. W. H. Lewis; and *The Added Dimension: The Art and Mind of Flannery O'Connor,* ed. Melvin J. Friedman and Lewis A. Lawson [New York: Fordham University Press, 1966]), *Report* 4 (January 1967): 32.

[6] "Flannery O'Connor," *Jubilee* 12 (November 1964): 53.

[7] *South Atlantic Quarterly* 55 (January 1956): 59.

[8] Hawkes's essay appeared in *Sewanee Review* 70 (Summer 1962): 395–407. Scott's essay, "Flannery O'Connor's Testimony: The Pressure of Glory," appeared in *The Added Dimension,* pp. 138–56.

[9] *New York Times Book Review* (25 May 1969): 7.

[10] *The Added Dimension,* p. 141. In many ways Scott is ideally suited to criticize Miss O'Connor's work, for he brings to it a long and distinguished career in the study of theology and literature. His emphasis in "Flannery O'Connor's Testimony" is theological; he views Miss O'Connor's novels largely as illustrative of an artistic tradition opposed to "profanization of life," or "desacralization." Heschel's book was

edited by Fritz A. Rothschild (New York: Harper & Row, 1959). Scott quotes pp. 38, 46, 54, and 45.

[11] *Esprit* 8 (Winter 1964): 13–14.

[12] George Lensing, in "De Chardin's Ideas in Flannery O'Connor," *Renascence* 18 (Summer 1966): 171–75, examines the humor of Miss O'Connor's works.

[13] Quoted in Robert Scholes, *The Fabulators* (New York: Oxford University Press), p. 59.

Chapter Two

[1] Quoted in John Hawkes, "Flannery O'Connor's Devil," *Sewanee Review* 70 (Summer 1962): 395.

[2] Quoted in James F. Light, *Nathanael West* (Evanston, Ill.: Northwestern University Press, 1961). See also West's "Some Notes on *Miss Lonely Hearts*," *Contempo* (15 May 1933): 2.

[3] "Some Notes on *Miss Lonely Hearts*," p. 2. See also West's "Some Notes on Violence," *Contact* (October 1932): 132.

[4] *Jubilee* 9 (May 1961): 28–35. The nuns' book bears Miss O'Connor's name on the title page. Thus far the introduction has been accorded little attention, possibly because critics assume it is but a pious, even sectarian, gesture.

[5] *Mosses from an Old Manse* (New York: A. L. Burt, ca. 1892), p. 199.

[6] *The Marble Faun* (New York: Standard Book Co., 1931), p. 288.

[7] *The Scarlet Letter* (Cambridge, Mass.: Houghton Mifflin Co., The Riverside Press, n.d.), pp. 30–31.

[8] *Twice-Told Tales* (New York: Standard Book Co., 1931), pp. 139–40, 141–42.

[9] *The Eccentric Design* (New York: Columbia University Press, 1963), p. 124.

[10] Published as "The Modern Novel: The Example of Mauriac," *Agora* 1 (1961): 18–24. The quotation appears on p. 23.

[11] *The Weakling* and *The Enemy*, 2 vols. in 1 (New York: Pellegrine and Cudahy, 1952), pp. 218–19. Subsequent citations to these two novels are to this edition.

Chapter Three

[1] *Everything That Rises Must Converge* (New York: Noonday Press, 1966), p. xviii. Subsequent citations to this collection are to this paperback edition.

[2] Sullivan made this criticism in his appraisal of *Everything That Rises Must Converge*, in *Hollins Critic* 2 (September 1965): 2.

[3] Melvin J. Friedman, "Flannery O'Connor: Another Legend in Southern Fiction," in *Recent American Fiction: Some Critical Views*, ed. Joseph J. Waldmeir (Boston: Houghton Mifflin, 1963), pp. 231–45.

[4] *3 by Flannery O'Connor* (New York: Signet, 1964), p. 9. This paperback edition includes *Wise Blood*, *A Good Man Is Hard to Find*, and *The Violent Bear It Away*. Subsequent citations to these three works are to this edition.

[5] Yeats is the only writer to whom Miss O'Connor referred directly in her fiction. In "The Enduring Chill" the protagonist sarcastically identifies a reference to Yeats in a letter to his mother.

Chapter Four

[1] Stanley Edgar Hyman has observed the appropriateness of his destination in *Flannery O'Connor,* University of Minnesota Pamphlets on American Writers, no. 54 (Minneapolis, Minn.: University of Minnesota Press, 1966), p. 19. Subsequent quotations from this study are cited by page.

[2] "Strange Earth: The Stories of Flannery O'Connor," *Georgia Review* 12 (Summer 1958): 215–22.

[3] Introduction to *A Memoir of Mary Ann; Mystery and Manners,* p. 228.

[4] Quoted in Eugene Murphy, "The Modern Novel: The Example of Mauriac," *Agora* 1 (1961): 24.

[5] *The True Country: Themes in the Fiction of Flannery O'Connor* (Nashville, Tenn.: Vanderbilt University Press, 1969), p. 174.

Chapter Five

[1] Quoted in Granville Hicks, "A Writer at Home with Her Heritage," *Saturday Review* 45 (12 May 1962): 22.

[2] "Flannery O'Connor's *The Violent Bear It Away*: Apotheosis in Failure," *Sewanee Review* 76 (Spring 1968): 319–36. The passages quoted appear on pp. 334, 335, 336.

Chapter Six

[1] "Parker's Back" originally appeared in *Esquire* (April 1965). "The Partridge Festival" appeared in *Critic* 19 (February–March 1961): 20–23, 82–85; subsequent citations to "The Partridge Festival" are to this publication.

[2] *Signs and Symbols of Christian Art* (New York: Oxford University Press, 1961), p. 22.

[3] "Flannery O'Connor's 'Parker's Back,' " *Renascence* 20 (Spring 1968): 164.

[4] "The Role of the Catholic Novelist," *Greyfriar* 7 (1963): 12.

[5] Philip Wheelwright, "Poetry, Myth, and Reality," in *The Modern Critical Spectrum,* ed. Gerald Jay Goldberg and Nancy Marmer Goldberg (Englewood Cliffs, N.J.: Prentice-Hall, 1965), p. 307.

[6] *The Future of Man* (New York: Harper & Row, 1964), p. 309.

[7] *The Divine Milieu,* rev. English ed. (New York: Harper & Row, 1965), p. 57.

[8] "O'Connor and Teilhard de Chardin: The Problem of Evil," *Renascence* 22 (Autumn 1969): 40, 41.

[9] "Convergence of Flannery O'Connor and Chardin," *Renascence* 19 (Fall 1966): 46.

[10] *All the King's Men* (New York: Random House, 1953), p. 464.

Bibliography

I. Flannery O'Connor's Fiction

1946
"The Geranium." *Accent* 6 (Summer): 245–53.

1948
"The Train." *Sewanee Review* 56 (April): 261–71. Later altered for chapter one, *Wise Blood.*

"The Capture." *Mademoiselle* 28 (November): 148–49, 195–96, 198–201.

1949
"The Heart of the Park." *Partisan Review* 16 (February): 138–51. Later altered for chapter five, *Wise Blood.*

"The Woman on the Stairs." *Tomorrow* 8 (August): 40. Later retitled "A Stroke of Good Fortune" in *Shenandoah* 4 (Spring 1953), and in *A Good Man Is Hard to Find* (1955).

"The Peeler." *Partisan Review* 16 (December): 1189–1206. Later altered for chapter three, *Wise Blood.*

1952
"Enoch and the Gorilla." *New World Writing* 1 (April): 67–74. Later altered for chapters eleven and twelve, *Wise Blood.*

Wise Blood. New York: Harcourt, Brace. British edition, London: Neville Spearman, 1955. Paperback edition, New York: Signet, June 1953.

1953
"A Stroke of Good Fortune." *Shenandoah* 4 (Spring): 7–18.

"The Life You Save May Be Your Own." *Kenyon Review* 15 (Spring): 195–207. Also published in *Perspectives USA* 14 (1956): 64–75; *Prize Stories 1954: The O. Henry Awards,* edited by Paul Engle and Hansford Martin, Garden City, N.Y.: Doubleday, 1954; *Prospetti,* Rome: Casa Editrice Sansoni, 1956.

"The River." *Sewanee Review* 61 (Summer): 455–75.

"A Late Encounter with the Enemy." *Harper's Bazaar* 87 (September): 234, 247, 249, 252.

"A Good Man Is Hard to Find." In *The Berkeley Book of Modern Writing*, vol. 1, edited by William Phillips and Phillip Rahv. New York: Berkeley Publishing Corp.: 1953. Pp. 186–99. Also published in *The House of Fiction*, edited by Caroline Gordon and Allen Tate, pp. 370–81. 2d ed. New York: Charles Scribner's Sons, 1960.

1954

"A Temple of the Holy Ghost." *Harper's Bazaar* 88 (May): 634–54.

"A Circle in the Fire." *Kenyon Review* 16 (Spring): 169–90. Also published in *The Best American Short Stories of 1955*, edited by Martha Foley, Boston: Houghton Mifflin, 1955; *Prize Stories 1955: The O. Henry Awards*, edited by Paul Engle and Hansford Martin, Garden City, N.Y.: Doubleday, 1955 (second prize story).

"The Displaced Person." *Sewanee Review* 62 (October): 634–54.

1955

"The Artificial Nigger." *Kenyon Review* 17 (Spring): 169–92. Also published in *The Best American Short Stories of 1956*, edited by Martha Foley, Boston: Houghton Mifflin, 1956; *Fiction of the Fifties*, edited by Herbert Gold, pp. 283–304, Garden City, N.Y.: Doubleday, 1959.

"Good Country People." *Harper's Bazaar* 89 (June): 64–65, 116–17, 121–22, 124, 130.

"You Can't Be Any Poorer than Dead." *New World Writing* 8 (October): 81–97.

A Good Man Is Hard to Find and Other Stories. New York: Harcourt, Brace. First collection of short stories, including:

"A Good Man Is Hard to Find"
"The River"
"The Life You Save May Be Your Own"
"A Stroke of Good Fortune"
"A Temple of the Holy Ghost"
"The Artificial Nigger"
"A Circle in the Fire"
"Good Country People"
"The Displaced Person"

Paperback edition, New York: Signet, October 1956, April 1961.

1956

"Greenleaf." *Kenyon Review* 18 (Summer): 384–410. Also published in *Prize Stories 1957: The O. Henry Awards*, edited by Paul Engle and Constance Urdang, Garden City, N.Y.: Doubleday, 1957 (first prize story); *The Best American Short Stories, 1919–1957*, edited by Martha Foley, Boston: Houghton, Mifflin, 1957; *First Prize Stories 1919–1963*, Garden City, N.Y.: Doubleday, 1963.

1957
"A View of the Woods." *Partisan Review* 24 (Fall): 475–596. Also published in *The Best American Short Stories of 1958*, edited by Martha Foley and David Burnett, Boston: Houghton Mifflin, 1958; *Prize Stories 1959: The O. Henry Awards*, edited by Paul Engle, Curt Harnack, and Constance Urdang, Garden City, N.Y.: Doubleday, 1959.

1958
"The Enduring Chill." *Harper's Bazaar* 91 (July): 44–45, 94, 96, 100–102, 108.

1960
"The Comforts of Home." *Kenyon Review* 22 (Fall): 523–46.
The Violent Bear It Away. New York: Farrar, Straus and Cudahy.

1961
"The Partridge Festival." *Critic* 19 (February-March): 20–23, 82–85.
"Everything That Rises Must Converge." *New World Writing* 20 (1961): 74–90. Also published in *The Best American Short Stories, 1962*, edited by Martha Foley, Boston: Houghton Mifflin, 1962; *First Prize Stories 1919–1963*, Garden City, N.Y.: Doubleday, 1963; *Prize Stories 1963: The O. Henry Awards*, edited by Richard Poirier, Garden City, N.Y.: Doubleday, 1963.

1962
"The Lame Shall Enter First." *Sewanee Review* 70 (Summer): 337–79.
Reissue of *Wise Blood*.

1963
"Why Do Heathens Rage?" *Esquire* 60 (July): 60–61. Excerpt from uncompleted third novel.

1964
"Revelation." *Sewanee Review* 72 (Spring): 178–202. Also published in *Prize Stories 1965: The O. Henry Awards*, edited by Richard Poirier and William Abraham, Garden City, N.Y.: Doubleday, 1965.
3 by Flannery O'Connor. New York: Signet. Paperback edition of *Wise Blood, A Good Man Is Hard to Find*, and *The Violent Bear It Away*.

1965
"Parker's Back." *Esquire* 63 (April): 76–78, 151–55.
Everything That Rises Must Converge. New York: Farrar, Straus and Giroux. Posthumous collection of short stories, including:
    "Everything That Rises Must Converge"
    "Greenleaf"
    "A View of the Woods"
    "The Enduring Chill"

"The Comforts of Home"
"The Lame Shall Enter First"
"Revelation"
"Parker's Back"
"Judgement Day" (first publication)

II. *Flannery O'Connor's Criticism and Nonfiction*

"Fiction Is a Subject with a History—It Should Be Taught That Way."
Georgia Bulletin (21 March 1963): 1. Later published as "Total Effect
and the Eighth Grade" in *Flannery O'Connor, Mystery and Manners:
Occasional Prose.*

Flannery O'Connor, Mystery and Manners: Occasional Prose. Selected
and edited by Sally and Robert Fitzgerald. New York: Farrar, Straus
and Giroux, 1969. Included in collection are.

  "The King of the Birds" (previously published as "Living with a Pea-
    cock")
  "The Fiction Writer and His Country" (previously published in *The
    Living Novel: A Symposium*)
  "Southern Fiction"
  "The Regional Writer" (previously published in *Esprit*)
  "The Nature and Aim of Fiction"
  "Writing Short Stories"
  "On Her Own Work"
  "The Teaching of Literature"
  "Total Effect and the Eighth Grade" (previously published as "Fiction
    Is a Subject with a History")
  "The Church and the Fiction Writer"
  "Novelist and Believer"
  "Catholic Novelists and Their Readers" (previously published as "The
    Role of the Catholic Novelist")
  "The Catholic Novelist in the Protestant South"
  "Introduction to *A Memoir of Mary Ann*" (previously published as
    "Mary Ann: The Story of a Little Girl")

"Living with a Peacock." *Holiday* 30 (September 1961): 523. Later published as "The King of the Birds" in *Flannery O'Connor, Mystery and
Manners: Occasional Prose.*

"Mary Ann: The Story of a Little Girl." *Jubilee* 9 (May 1961): 28–35.
Condensed for *Family Digest* 17 (May 1962): 36–50. Also published as
introduction to *A Memoir of Mary Ann.* New York: Farrar, Straus and
Cudahy, 1961.

"Replies to Two Questions." *Esprit* 3 (Winter 1959): 10.

Review of *The Phenomenon of Man. American Scholar* 30 (Fall 1961): 618.

"Some Aspects of the Grotesque in Southern Literature." *Cluster Review,* (Mercer University, Macon, Ga., March 1965): 5, 6, 22.

"The Church and the Fiction Writer." *America* 46 (30 March 1957): 733–35.

"The Fiction Writer and His Country." In *The Living Novel: A Symposium,* edited by Granville Hicks, pp. 157–64. New York: Macmillan, 1957. Later published in *Flannery O'Connor, Mystery and Manners: Occasional Prose.*

"The Mystery of Suffering." *Catholic Mind* 60 (February 1962): 23–29.

"The Novelist and Free Will." *Fresco* (University of Detroit, Winter 1963): 31–35.

"The Regional Writer." *Esprit* 7 (Winter 1963): 31–35.

"The Role of the Catholic Novelist." *Greyfriar* 7 (1963): 5–12. Later published (partially) in *Flannery O'Connor, Mystery and Manners: Occasional Prose* as "Catholic Novelists and Their Readers."

III. Biographical Articles

Adler, Johanna. "Author Flannery O'Connor . . . A Study in Contrast." *Raleigh Times* (12 April 1962).

Agnes, Sister. "In Memory of Flannery O'Connor." *America* 111 (17 October 1954): 455.

"An Interview with Flannery O'Connor." *Censer* (Fall 1960): 28–30.

"An Interview with Flannery O'Connor and Robert Penn Warren." *Vagabond* 4 (February 1960): 9–16.

Breit, Harvey. *New York Times* (12 June 1955). Portrait.

Coffee, Warren. "Flannery O'Connor." *Commentary* 40 (27 November 1965): 93–99.

Colby, Vineta. "Flannery O'Connor." *Wilson Library Bulletin* 32 (June 1958): 682.

Current Biography 26 (September 1965): 23. Obituary.

Daniel, Frank. "Flannery O'Connor Shapes Own Capital." *Atlanta Journal* and *Atlanta Constitution* (22 July 1962).

Esprit 8 (Winter 1964). Memorial edition.

Fitzgerald, Robert. Introduction to *Everything That Rises Must Converge.* New York: Farrar, Straus and Giroux, 1964.

———. Introduction to *Flannery O'Connor, Mystery and Manners: Occasional Prose.* New York: Farrar, Straus and Giroux, 1969.

"Frustrated Preacher." *Newsweek* 39 (19 May 1952): 114–15.

Georgia Bulletin (August 1964). Obituary.

Griffith, Albert. "Flannery O'Connor." *America* 113 (27 November 1965): 674–75.

Hallaman, Paul J. "Archbishop's Notebook." *Georgia Bulletin* (6 August 1964). Obituary.

Hicks, Granville. "A Writer at Home with Her Heritage." *Saturday Review* 45 (12 May 1962): 22–23.

Jubilee 11 (June 1963): 11. Interview.

Lockridge, Betsy. "An Afternoon with Flannery O'Connor." *Atlanta Journal* and *Atlanta Constitution* (1 November 1959).

Mary Alice, Sister. "My Mentor, Flannery O'Connor." *Saturday Review* 48 (29 May 1965): 24–25.

Mayhew, L. F. S. "Flannery O'Connor: 1925–1964." *Commonweal* 80 (21 August 1964): 562–63.

Merton, Thomas. "Flannery O'Connor." *Jubilee* 12 (November 1964): 53.

"Motley Special: An Interview with Flannery O'Connor." *Motley* (Spring 1959): 29–31.

Mullins, C. Ross, Jr. "Flannery O'Connor: An Interview." *Jubilee* 11 (June 1963): 32–35.

New York Times (4 August 1964). Obituary.

Publishers Weekly (17 August 1964): 28. Obituary.

Roseliep, Raymond. "Flannery O'Connor, 1925–1964." *Georgia Review* 19 (Fall 1965): 368.

Schott, Warren. "Flannery O'Connor: Faith's Stepchild." *Nation* 201 (13 September 1965): 142–44.

Sherry, Gerard. "An Interview with Flannery O'Connor." *Critic* 21 (June-July 1963): 29–31.

"Southern Writers Are Stuck with the South." *Atlanta* (August 1963): 26.

Stern, Richard. "Flannery O'Connor: A Remembrance and Some Letters." *Shenandoah* 16 (Winter 1965): 5–10.

Taillefer, Anne. "A Memoir of Flannery O'Connor." *Catholic Worker* 31 (December 1964): 24.

Time (14 August 1964): 59. Obituary.

Turner, Margaret. "Visit to Flannery O'Connor Proves a Novel Experience." *Atlanta Journal* and *Atlanta Constitution* (29 May 1960).

Wells, Joel. "Conversation with Flannery O'Connor." *Critic* 21 (August-September 1962): 5.

IV. Criticism and Reviews

Adams, R. M. "Fiction Chronicle." *Hudson Review* 8 (Winter 1956): 630.

Aldridge, John W. *In Search of Heresy*. New York: McGraw Hill, 1956.

Alpert, Hollis. "Coterie Tales." *Saturday Review* 40 (19 January 1957): 42.

Alvis, John. *"Wise Blood*: Hope in the City of the Profane." *Kerygma* 4 (Winter 1965): 18–29.

America 102 (5 March 1960): 682. Review of *The Violent Bear It Away*.

Ave Maria 92 (2 July 1960): 25. Review of *The Violent Bear It Away*.

Barrett, William. *Atlantic* 216 (July 1965): 139. Review of *Everything That Rises Must Converge*.

Bassan, Maurice. "Flannery O'Connor's Way: Shock with Moral Intent." *Renascence* 15 (Summer 1963): 195–99, 211.

Baumback, Jonathan. "The Acid of God's Grace: The Fiction of Flannery O'Connor." *Georgia Review* 17 (Fall 1963): 334–46.

Bertrande, Sister. "Four Stories of Flannery O'Connor." *Thought* 37 (Fall 1962): 410–26.

Bone, L. E. *Library Journal* 90 (1 May 1965): 2160. Review of *Everything That Rises Must Converge*.

Booklist 61 (15 June 1955): 428. Review of *A Good Man Is Hard to Find*.

Booklist 66 (1 April 1960): 478. Review of *The Violent Bear It Away*.

Bookmark 14 (July 1955): 246. Review of *A Good Man Is Hard to Find*.

Bordwell, Harold. "The Fiction of Flannery O'Connor: Her Work." *Today* 21 (October 1965): 29.

Bornhauser, Fred. *Shenandoah* 7 (Autumn 1955): 71–81. Review of *A Good Man Is Hard to Find*.

Bowen, Robert O. "Hope versus Despair in the Gothic Novel." *Renascence* 13 (Spring 1961): 147–52.

Bradbury, John M. *Renaissance in the South: A Critical History of the Literature, 1920–1960*. Chapel Hill, N.C.: University of North Carolina Press, 1963.

Brittain, Joan T. "Flannery O'Connor: A Bibliography, Part 1." *Bulletin of Bibliography* 25 (September-December 1967): 98–100.

———. "Flannery O'Connor: A Bibliography, Part 2." *Bulletin of Bibliography* 25 (January-April 1968): 123–24.

———. "Flannery O'Connor: A Bibliography, Addenda." *Bulletin of Bibliography* 25 (May-August 1968): 142.

———. "Flannery O'Connor's *A Good Man Is Hard to Find*." *Explicator* 26 (September 1967): item 1.

———. "Symbols of Violence: Flannery O'Connor's Structure of Reality." Master's thesis, University of Louisville, 1966.

———. "The Fictional Family of Flannery O'Connor." *Renascence* 19 (Fall 1966): 48–52.

Brittain, Joan T., and Driskell, Leon V. "O'Connor and the Eternal Cross-roads." *Renascence* 22 (Autumn 1969): 48–55.

Burns, Stuart L. "Flannery O'Connor's Literary Apprenticeship." *Renascence* 22 (Autumn 1969): 3–16.

———. "Flannery O'Connor's *The Violent Bear It Away*: Apotheosis in Failure." *Sewanee Review* 76 (Spring 1968): 319–36.

Butcher, Fanny. *Chicago Sunday Tribune* (3 July 1955). Review of *A Good Man Is Hard to Find*.

Byam, M. L. *Library Journal* 77 (15 May 1952): 894. Review of *Wise Blood*.

Canfield, Francis. *Critic* 18 (May 1960): 45. Review of *The Violent Bear It Away*.

Carter, Thomas H. *Accent* 15 (Autumn 1955): 293–97. Review of *A Good Man Is Hard to Find*.

Charles, Gerda. *New Statesman* 60 (24 September 1960): 445. Review of *The Violent Bear It Away*.

Cheney, Brainard. "Flannery O'Connor's Campaign for Her Country." *Sewanee Review* 72 (Autumn 1964): 555–58.

———. "Miss O'Connor Creates Unusual Humor out of Ordinary Sin." *Sewanee Review* 71 (Autumn 1963): 644–52.

Christian Century 77 (1 June 1960): 672. Review of *The Violent Bear It Away*.

Critic 21 (November 1962): 95. Review of *Wise Blood*.

Daniel, Frank. "Good Writer Must Set His Book in a Region Which Is Familiar." *Atlanta Journal* (28 March 1960).

Davenport, Guy. *National Review* 17 (27 July 1965): 658. Review of *Everything That Rises Must Converge*.

Davidson, Donald. "A Prophet Went Forth." *New York Times Book Review* (28 February 1960): 4. Review of *The Violent Bear It Away*.

Davis, Barnabas. "Flannery O'Connor: Christian Belief in Recent Fiction." *Listening* (Autumn 1965): 5–19.

Davis, Joe Lee. "Outraged or Embarrassed." *Kenyon Review* 16 (Spring 1953): 320–26.

Degnan, James P. *Commonweal* 82 (9 July 1965): 510–11. Review of *Everything That Rises Must Converge*.

Detweiler, Robert. "The Curse of Christ in Flannery O'Connor's Fiction." *Comparative Literary Studies* 2 (1965): 235–45.

Donner, Robert. "She Writes Powerful Fiction." *Sign* 40 (March 1961): 46–48.

Dowell, Robert. "The Moment of Grace in the Fiction of Flannery O'Connor." *College English* 7 (December 1965): 235–39.

Drake, Robert. *Christian Century* 82 (19 May 1965): 656. Review of *Everything That Rises Must Converge.*

———. "The Bleeding, Stinking Mad Shadow of Jesus in the Fiction of Flannery O'Connor." *Comparative Literary Studies* 2 (1965): 183–96.

———. "The Harrowing Evangel of Flannery O'Connor." *Christian Century* 81 (30 September 1964): 1200–1202.

Driskell, Leon V. "Flannery O'Connor: Property of Specialists? A Review of *Mystery and Manners* and *The True Country.*" *Louisville Courier-Journal and Times* (15 June 1969).

———. " ' Parker's Back' vs. 'The Partridge Festival': Flannery O'Connor's Critical Choice." *Georgia Review* 21 (Winter 1967): 476–90.

Duhamel, P. Albert. "Flannery O'Connor's Violent View of Reality." *Catholic World* 190 (February 1960): 280–85.

Dupree, Robert. "The Fictional World of Flannery O'Connor." *Kerygma* 4 (Winter 1965): 3–18.

Elder, Walter. "That Region." *Kenyon Review* 17 (Autumn 1955): 661–70.

Emerson, D. C. *Arizona Quarterly* 16 (Autumn 1960): 284–86. Review of *The Violent Bear It Away.*

Engle, Paul. *Chicago Sunday Tribune* (6 March 1960). Review of *The Violent Bear It Away.*

Esty, William. "The Gratuitous Grotesque." *Commonweal* 67 (7 March 1958): 586–88.

Extension 55 (July 1960): 26. Review of *The Violent Bear It Away.*

Fahey, William A. "Flannery O'Connor's 'Parker's Back.' " *Renascence* 20 (Spring 1968): 162–64, 166.

Farnham, James F. "O'Connor's *Everything That Rises Must Converge.*" *Cross Currents* 15 (Summer 1965): 376.

———. "The Grotesque in Flannery O'Connor." *America* 105 (13 May 1961): 277–81.

Ferris, Sumner J. "The Outside and the Inside: Flannery O'Connor's *The Violent Bear It Away.*" *Critique* 3 (Winter-Spring 1960): 11–19.

Fitzgerald, Robert. "The Countryside and the True Country." *Sewanee Review* 70 (Summer 1962): 380–94.

Freeman, Warren Eugene, S.J. "The Social and Theological Implications in Flannery O'Connor's *A Good Man Is Hard to Find.*" Master's thesis, University of North Carolina, 1962.

Fremantle, Anne. *Commonweal* 75 (16 February 1962): 545. Review of "A Memoir of Mary Ann."

Friedman, Melvin J. "Flannery O'Connor: Another Legend in Southern Fiction." *English Journal: The High School Organ of the National*

Council of Teachers of English 51 (April 1962): 233–43. Also published in *Recent American Fiction: Some Critical Views.* Edited by Joseph J. Waldmeir. Boston: Houghton Mifflin, 1963.

Friedman, Melvin J., and Lawson, Lewis A., eds. *The Added Dimension: The Art and Mind of Flannery O'Connor.* New York: Fordham University Press, 1966. Work also includes articles by Norman Charles, Albert Duhamel, Harold Gardner, Caroline Gordon, Frederich Hoffman, Hugh Holman, Irving Malin, Flannery O'Connor, Bernetta Quinn, Louis Rubin, Nathan Scott, and William Sessions.

Gable, Sister Mariella. *Critic* 23 (June-July 1965): 58. Review of *Everything That Rises Must Converge.*

———. "Ecumenical Core in Flannery O'Connor's Fiction." *American Benedictine Review* 15 (June 1964): 127–43.

Gafford, Charlotte. "The Fiction of Flannery O'Connor: A Mission of Gratuitous Grace." Master's thesis, Birmingham Southern College, 1962.

Gardner, Harold. *America* 106 (13 January 1962): 474. Review of "A Memoir of Mary Ann."

"God Breaks Through." *America* 112 (5 July 1965): 821.

"God Intoxicated Hillbillies." *Time* 75 (29 February 1960): 188, 221.

Gordon, Caroline. "Flannery O'Connor's *Wise Blood.*" *Critique* 2 (Fall 1958): 3–10.

———. "Heresy in Dixie." *Sewanee Review* 76 (Spring 1968): 261–97.

———. *New York Times* (12 June 1955): 5. Review of *A Good Man Is Hard to Find.*

Gordon, Caroline, and Tate, Allen, eds. *The House of Fiction: An Anthology of the Short Story with Commentary.* 2d ed. New York: Charles Scribner's Sons, 1960.

Gossett, Louise Y. *Violence in Recent Southern Fiction.* Durham, N.C.: Duke University Press, 1965.

Gossett, T. F. *Southwest Review* 46 (Winter 1961): 87. Review of *The Violent Bear It Away.*

Goyen, William. *New York Times* (18 May 1952). Review of *Wise Blood.*

Grail 38 (January 1956): 59. Review of *A Good Man Is Hard to Find.*

Griffith, Albert. "Flannery O'Connor." *America* 113 (27 November 1965): 674–75.

Hawkes, John. "Flannery O'Connor's Devil." *Sewanee Review* 70 (Summer 1962): 395–407.

———. "Notes on the Wild Goose Chase." *Massachusetts Review* 3 (Summer 1962): 784–88.

———. "Scholars, Critics, Writers and the Campus." *Wisconsin Studies in Contemporary Literature* 6 (Summer 1965): 146–47.

Hicks, Granville. "A Cold, Hard Look at Humankind." *Saturday Review* 48 (29 May 1965): 23–24.

——. "Holy Kind of Horror." *Saturday Review* 49 (2 July 1966): 21–22.

——. *Saturday Review* 43 (27 February 1960): 18. Review of *The Violent Bear It Away*.

Hoobler, Thomas. "*Everything That Rises Must Converge*: A Review." *Ave Maria* 102 (17 July 1965): 18.

Hoskins, Frank. "Editor's Comments." *Studies in Short Fiction* 2 (Fall 1964): iii–iv.

Hughes, Riley. *Catholic World* 182 (October 1955): 66. Review of *A Good Man Is Hard to Find*.

Hyman, Stanley Edgar. *Flannery O'Connor*. University of Minnesota Pamphlets on American Writers, no. 54. Minneapolis, Minn.: University of Minnesota Press, 1966.

Information 74 (April 1960): 57. Review of *The Violent Bear It Away*.

Jacobsen, Josephine. "A Catholic Quartet." *Christian Scholar* 47 (Summer 1964): 139–54.

Jeremy, Sister. "*The Violent Bear It Away*: A Linguistic Education." *Renascence* 17 (Fall 1964): 11–16.

Jones, Bartlett C. "Depth Psychology and Literary Study." *Midcontinent American Studies Journal* 1 (Fall 1964): 50–56.

Joselyn, Sister M. "Thematic Centers in 'The Displaced Person.'" *Studies in Short Fiction* 1 (Winter 1964): 85–92.

Kevin, Sister Mary, O.S.B. "Flannery O'Connor: In Memory of a Vision Unlimited." *Censer* (Winter 1965): 37–42.

Kieft, Ruth M. Vande. "Judgment in the Fiction of Flannery O'Connor." *Sewanee Review* 76 (Spring 1968): 337–56.

Kiely, Robert. *Christian Science Monitor* 57 (17 June 1965): 7. Review of *Everything That Rises Must Converge*.

Kirkus 20 (1 May 1952): 285. Review of *Wise Blood*.

Kirkus 23 (15 April 1955): 290. Review of *A Good Man Is Hard to Find*.

Kirkus 27 (15 December 1959): 931. Review of *The Violent Bear It Away*.

Kirkus 33 (15 March 1965): 338. Review of *Everything That Rises Must Converge*.

LaFarge, Oliver. "Manic Gloom." *Saturday Review* 35 (24 May 1952): 22.

Lawson, Lewis Allen. "Flannery O'Connor and the Grotesque: *Wise Blood*." *Renascence* 17 (Spring 1965): 137–47, 156.

LeClezio, J. M. G. "L'univers de Flannery O'Connor." *Nouvelle Revue Francaise* 13 (September 1965): 488–93.

Lensing, George. "De Chardin's Ideas in Flannery O'Connor." *Renascence* 18 (Summer 1966): 171–75.

Levine, Paul. "The Violent Art." *Jubilee* 10 (December 1962): 47. Review of *Wise Blood*.

Lewis, R. W. *Hudson Review* 6 (Spring 1953): 144–50. Review of *Wise Blood*.

Lodge, David. *Tablet* 214 (17 December 1960): 1175. Review of *The Violent Bear It Away*.

Lorch, T. M. "Flannery O'Connor: Christian Allegorist." *Critique* 10 (1968): 69–80.

Ludwig, Jack B. In *Recent American Novelists*, pp. 36–37. University of Mississippi Pamphlets on American Writers, no. 22. Jackson, Miss., 1962.

McCarthy, John. "Human Intelligence vs. Divine Truth: The Intellectual in Flannery O'Connor's Works." *English Journal* 50 (December 1966): 1143–48.

McCown, Robert, S.J. "Flannery O'Connor and the Reality of Sin." *Catholic World* 188 (January 1959): 285 91.

———. "The Education of a Prophet: A Study of Flannery O'Connor's *The Violent Bear It Away*." *Kansas Magazine* (1962): 73–78.

Malin, Irving. *New American Gothic*. Carbondale, Ill.: Southern Illinois University Press, 1962.

Marshall, J. D. "Flannery O'Connor." *Library Journal* 80 (15 May 1955): 1217. Review of *A Good Man Is Hard to Find*.

Martin, Carter W. *The True Country: Themes in the Fiction of Flannery O'Connor*. Nashville, Tenn.: Vanderbilt University Press, 1969.

Martin, Sister M. "O'Connor's 'A Good Man Is Hard to Find.'" *Explicator* 24 (October 1965): item 19.

Meaders, M. J. "Literary Witch." *Colorado Quarterly* 10 (Spring 1962): 377–86.

Meeker, Richard K. "The Youngest Generation of Southern Fiction Writers." *Southern Writers* (University of Virginia, 1964): 186–87.

"Memento Mori." *Times Literary Supplement* (24 March 1966): 242.

Meyers, Sister Bertrande, D.C. "Four Stories of Flannery O'Connor." *Thought* 37 (Autumn 1962): 410–26.

Modern Age 4 (Fall 1960): 428–30. Review of *The Violent Bear It Away*.

Montgomery, Marion. "O'Connor and Teilhard de Chardin: The Problem of Evil." *Renascence* 22 (Autumn 1969): 34–42.

———. "The Sense of Violation: Notes toward a Definition of Southern Fiction." *Georgia Review* 19 (Fall 1965): 278–87.

Muggeridge, Malcolm. *Esquire* 63 (May 1965): 46. Review of *Everything That Rises Must Converge.*

Muller, Gilbert H. *"The Violent Bear It Away:* Moral and Dramatic Sense." *Renascence* 22 (Autumn 1969): 17–25.

Murray, James. "Southland *à la russe." Critic* 21 (July 1963): 26–28.

New Yorker 28 (14 June 1952): 118. Review of *Wise Blood.*

New Yorker 36 (15 March 1960): 179. Review of *The Violent Bear It Away.*

Newsweek 65 (31 May 1965): 85. Review of *Everything That Rises Must Converge.*

Nolde, Sister M. Simon, O.S.B. *"The Violent Bear It Away:* A Study in Imagery." *Xavier University Studies* 1 (Spring 1962): 180–94.

Nyren, Dorothy. *Library Journal* 85 (1 January 1960): 146. Review of *The Violent Bear It Away.*

Peden, William. *The American Short Story.* Boston: Houghton Mifflin, 1964.

Pritchett, V. S. "Satan Comes to Georgia." *New Statesman* 71 (1 April 1966): 469.

Quinn, John J. *Best Sellers* 19 (1 March 1960): 414. Review of *The Violent Bear It Away.*

———. *Best Sellers* 21 (15 December 1961): 394. Review of "A Memoir of Mary Ann."

———. *Best Sellers* 25 (1 June 1965): 124. Review of *Everything That Rises Must Converge.*

Quinn, Sister M. Bernetta. "View from a Rock: The Fiction of Flannery O'Connor and J. F. Powers." *Critique* 2 (Fall 1958): 19–27.

Quinn, Thomas. "Lewis and O'Connor: Prophets of the Added Dimension." *Report* 4 (January 1967): 32–33. Review of *Letters* of C. S. Lewis, ed. W. H. Lewis, and *The Added Dimension: The Art and Mind of Flannery O'Connor,* ed. Melvin J. Friedman and Lewis A. Lawson.

Ragan, Marjorie. "Southern Accent." *Raleigh Times* (18 April 1965).

Rechnitz, Robert M. "Passionate Pilgrim: Flannery O'Connor's *Wise Blood." Georgia Review* 19 (Fall 1965): 310–16.

Rose Alice, Sister, S.S.J. "Flannery O'Connor: Poet to the Outcast." *Renascence* 16 (Spring 1964): 126–32.

Roseliep, Raymond. "Flannery O'Connor, 1925–1964." *Georgia Review* 19 (Fall 1965): 368.

Rosenberger, Coleman. *New York Herald Tribune Weekly Book Review* (28 February 1960): 23. Review of *The Violent Bear It Away.*

Rosenfeld, Isaac. *New Republic* 127 (7 July 1952): 19. Review of *Wise Blood.*

Rubin, Louis D., Jr. "Flannery O'Connor: A Note on Literary Fashions." *Critique* 2 (Fall 1958): 11–18.

———. *The Faraway Country*. Seattle, Wash.: University of Washington Press, 1963.

———. "Two Ladies of the South." *Sewanee Review* 63 (Autumn 1955): 671–81.

Rupp, Richard H. "Flannery O'Connor." *Commonweal* 79 (December 1963): 304–7.

San Francisco Chronicle (25 February 1960). Review of *The Violent Bear It Away*.

Saturday Review 40 (19 January 1957): 42. Review of *Prize Stories 1957* ("Greenleaf").

Sessions, William. "Flannery O'Connor: A Memoir." *National Catholic Reporter* (28 October 1964): 9.

Shear, Walter. "Flannery O'Connor: Character and Characterization." *Renascence* 20 (Spring 1968): 140–46.

Simons, J. W. "A Case of Possession." *Commonweal* 61 (27 June 1952): 297–98. Review of *Wise Blood*.

Smith, J. Oates. "Ritual and Violence in Flannery O'Connor." *Thought* 41 (Winter 1966): 545–60.

Snow, Ollye Tine. "The Functional Gothic of Flannery O'Connor." *Southwest Review* 50 (Summer 1965): 286–99.

Solotaroff, Theodore. *Book Week* (30 May 1965): 1. Review of *Everything That Rises Must Converge*.

Spivey, Ted. "Flannery O'Connor's View of God and Man." *Studies in Short Fiction* 1 (Spring 1964): 200–206.

Springfield Republican (6 March 1960). Review of *The Violent Bear It Away*.

Stallings, Sylvia. "Flannery O'Connor: A New Shining Talent among Our Storytellers." *New York Herald Tribune Weekly Book Review* (5 June 1955): 1. Review of *A Good Man Is Hard to Find*.

Steggert, Frank X. *Books on Trial* 14 (December 1955): 187. Review of *A Good Man Is Hard to Find*.

Stelzman, Rainulf. "Der Stein des Anstosses: Die Romane und Erzählungen Flannery O'Connors." *Stimmen der Zeit* 174 (1964): 286–96.

———. "Shock and Orthodoxy: An Interpretation of Flannery O'Connor's Novels and Short Stories." *Xavier University Studies* 2 (March 1963): 4–21.

"Such Nice People." *Time* 65 (June 1955): 114. Review of *A Good Man Is Hard to Find*.

Sullivan, Walter. "Flannery O'Connor, Sin, and Grace: *Everything That Rises Must Converge*." *Hollins Critic* 2 (September 1965): 1–8, 10.

————. "The Continuing Renascence: Southern Fiction in the Fifties." In *South: Modern Southern Literature in its Cultural Setting,* edited by Louis D. Rubin, Jr., and Robert D. Jacobs. Garden City, N.Y.: Doubleday, 1961.

"The Novelist and Free Will." *Fresco* 1 (Winter 1961): 100–101.

Thomas, Esther. "Flannery O'Connor Helps Nuns Write Child's Story." *Atlanta Journal* (10 August 1961).

Thorp, Willard. "Suggs and Sut in Modern Dress." *Mississippi Quarterly* 13 (Fall 1960): 169–75.

Time 59 (9 June 1952): 108, 110. Review of *Wise Blood.*

Time 75 (29 February 1960): 118. Review of *The Violent Bear It Away.*

Time 85 (4 June 1965): 92. Review of *Everything That Rises Must Converge.*

Times Literary Supplement 2792 (2 September 1955): 505. Review of *Wise Blood.*

Trowbridge, Clinton W. "The Symbolic Vision of Flannery O'Connor: Patterns of Imagery in *The Violent Bear It Away.*" *Sewanee Review* 76 (Spring 1968): 298–318.

U.S. Quarterly Book Review 8 (Summer 1952): 256. Review of *Wise Blood.*

Virginia Quarterly Review 41 (Summer 1965): 150w. Review of *Everything That Rises Must Converge.*

Volger, Lewis. *San Francisco Chronicle* (10 July 1955). Review of *A Good Man Is Hard to Find.*

Walter, Sarah. "Strange Prophets of Flannery O'Connor." *Censer* (Spring 1960): 5–12.

Warnke, F. J. *New Republic* 142 (14 March 1960): 18. Review of *The Violent Bear It Away.*

Webster, Harvey C. "Nihilism as a Faith." *New Leader* 35 (23 June 1952): 23–24. Review of *Wise Blood.*

Wedge, George F. "Two Bibliographies: Flannery O'Connor, J. F. Powers." *Critique* 2 (Fall 1958): 59–63.

Wells, Joel. "Misfits in a Hung-over Biblical Land." *U.S. Catholic* 31 (July 1965): 62.

Wisconsin Library Bulletin 51 (July 1955): 11. Review of *A Good Man Is Hard to Find.*

Wyllie, J. C. *Saturday Review* 38 (4 June 1955): 15. Review of *A Good Man Is Hard to Find.*

Index